C.B. Bernard Mallet

Indian Finance

THREE ESSAYS,

(*Republished from the "Nineteenth Century,"*)

WITH AN INTRODUCTION AND APPENDIX.

BY

HENRY FAWCETT, M.P.,

FELLOW OF TRINITY HALL,

AND PROFESSOR OF POLITICAL ECONOMY IN THE UNIVERSITY OF CAMBRIDGE.

London:

MACMILLAN AND CO.

1880.

LONDON:
R. CLAY, SONS, AND TAYLOR, PRINTERS,
BREAD STREET HILL, E.C.

PREFACE.

The three Essays which form the chief contents of this volume were published last year in the *Nineteenth Century*, and I wish to express my best thanks to my friend, Mr. James Knowles, the Editor of that Review, for his kind courtesy in permitting their republication. In some introductory remarks I have endeavoured to show the importance of placing the present system of financial control on a different basis. Although it is generally supposed that the entire control over the expenditure of the revenues of India was vested in the Council of the Secretary of State by the Government of India Act of 1858, yet by an Act which was passed in 1869 the tenure of the office of the Members of Council was materially modified, and the discussion which took place when this Act was passing through Parliament plainly shows that the law had been left in a state of such extreme uncertainty by the Act of 1858 as to make inquiry into the entire subject by a Parliamentary Committee urgently necessary.

In a short Appendix to the last Essay, attention is directed to some important Amendments which, within the last few weeks, the Government of India have proposed to introduce into the Trades Licence-Tax, and some remarks are made on the intention which was at the same time expressed to relinquish the Famine Fund.

As I have always felt that Indian questions should as far as possible be discussed free from any party bias, I hope it will be found that none of the remarks contained in this volume have in any way been influenced by a feeling of political partisanship.

I desire to say how much I am indebted in the preparation of this book to my wife, who has revised the volume as it was passing through the press, and to my secretary, Mr. F. J. Dryhurst, who has acted as my amanuensis, and who has carefully verified the statistics which have been quoted from official and other documents.

HENRY FAWCETT.

CAMBRIDGE, *January* 21, 1880.

CONTENTS.

INDIAN FINANCE.

INTRODUCTORY REMARKS.

It is now generally recognised that no public question is of more urgent importance than the reform of Indian finance, and I have decided to republish the three essays contained in this volume, in the hope that they may possibly render some assistance in showing what is the true character of the financial condition of India, and what are the measures which it will be necessary to adopt to place her finances on a sound and satisfactory basis. In the first Essay, which was published in February last year, I endeavoured to describe the most salient features of the actual financial condition of India. Particular attention was directed in this essay to the erroneous conclusions which are frequently arrived at with regard to the amount of the real revenue which is available to meet the ordinary expenses of government. By arranging the various items of revenue and expenditure under different classes, and by carefully distinguishing the net from the gross receipts, it was shown that the real revenue of India is less than 40,000,000*l.*[1] With a comparatively stationary revenue of this amount, a rapidly-increasing expenditure had to be met. All available sources of taxation had been so nearly exhausted that large loans had each year to be raised to meet the deficits which were regularly accruing. Constant borrowing had consequently become the normal condition of Indian finance, and her indebtedness was rapidly and steadily growing. The budget for 1879–80, which was introduced at Calcutta soon after this Essay was published, strikingly corroborated the conclusions which were thus sought to be established. During this year the finances of India were prejudicially affected by various adverse circumstances. The cost of the Afghan war had to be met; an increasing loss by exchange, produced by the depreciation in the value of silver, put a severe strain upon her resources; various public works, which involved a heavy outlay, had already been sanctioned; the diminished revenue returns yielded in certain districts showed that in some parts of the country the effects of the recent famines were still severely felt; and the financial

[1] See table, p. 21.

situation was further aggravated by an increase in the military and other branches of expenditure. From the budget arrangements of the year it at once became evident that all the worst anticipations as to the financial exigencies of India were to receive a practical corroboration. In the second Essay, which was published in May, soon after these arrangements were made known, it was shown that the Government, from the measures which they proposed, apparently thought that India was so entirely without any financial reserve, and that all the sources of fresh taxation were so exhausted, that no effort could be made to obtain additional revenue. Consequently the whole of the exceptional expenditure could only be met by borrowing. The loan operations of the year were to be on so extended a scale that the critical state of Indian finance was at once disclosed, and on all sides the gravity of the situation was at length fully recognised. A loan of 3,500,000*l.* was to be raised in India; 2,000,000*l.* was to be advanced by England to India, free of interest, towards the expenses of the Afghan war; and soon after the budget was introduced at Calcutta, it was announced that the Government would ask Parliament for authority to borrow 10,000,000*l.* in England. But serious as was the state of things disclosed by these exceptionally large borrowing operations, the outlook for the future became far worse when it was seen that in the midst of this embarrassment the Government of India were surrounded by influences which compelled them, in the administration of her finances, to sacrifice her interests to the interests of England. Simultaneously with the announcement of the large loan operations which were about to be undertaken, it was stated that the revenue of India, which was admitted to be inadequate to meet the cost of government, was not to be maintained, but that 200,000*l.* of this revenue was to be sacrificed by a partial repeal of the cotton duties. It need scarcely be remarked that nothing can be more indefensible than to reduce taxes when there is a deficit, and when, consequently, every shilling of the taxation remitted necessitates a corresponding addition to the debt.

When the Indian budget was considered in Parliament (May 22, 1879), the Government made no attempt to conceal the extreme gravity of the financial situation. It was unreservedly admitted that as the revenue could not be added to by increased taxation, a reduction of expenditure became a matter of imperative necessity. In the last of the three Essays in this volume, which was published in October, I have endeavoured to show that this recognition by the Government of the true state of

Indian finance, and the promises with which it was accompanied of carrying out in every department a policy of the most rigorous economy, are so important that they may be regarded as constituting a new epoch in Indian finance. It is not too much to say that unless a policy of retrenchment is resolutely persisted in, nothing can prevent India being involved in the most serious financial embarrassment. All experience shows that any Government which attempts to carry out a policy of retrenchment will have to encounter many most formidable difficulties, and in surmounting these difficulties they may fairly claim all the assistance which public opinion can afford.

It will, I believe, be found that in order permanently to place the finances of India on a sound basis it will be necessary to effect some important changes in her present system of financial administration. It will now be generally admitted that when the Government of India was transferred from the Company to the Crown, many safeguards for economy were swept away, and the substitutes which took their place have proved to be comparatively ineffective.

It was perhaps impossible at the time the transfer took place to foresee many of the defects of the new system of government which was then introduced. As, however, more than twenty years have now elapsed since the commencement of this new system of administration, the time has, I think, arrived when great good would be likely to result if the Act of 1858, by which the transfer of the Government of India from the Company to the Crown was effected, and the amending Acts which have been subsequently passed, were subjected to a careful parliamentary inquiry. Among the many reasons that may be urged in favour of such an inquiry, it may be mentioned that the experience of the past has shown that it is in the highest degree desirable that Indian affairs should be periodically investigated. In the days of the Company such an investigation was insured at regular intervals, because the Charter of the Company, from which it derived its authority, was only granted for twenty years, and each renewal of the Charter was invariably preceded by a parliamentary inquiry. The three Committees which were thus appointed before the Charter was renewed in 1813, in 1833, and in 1853, collected information, the importance of which can hardly be overestimated. This was so fully recognised at the time when the Committees were appointed that many of the most eminent members of the House served upon them. The Committee which preceded the renewal of the Charter in 1813 first sat in 1808, and continued its sittings until 1812. During this time it made five reports. Among those who served on this

Committee may be mentioned Lord Castlereagh, Mr. Tierney, Mr. Wilberforce, Mr. Dundas, Mr. Charles Grant, the Duke of Wellington (then Sir Arthur Wellesley), and Sir Robert Peel. The next Committee was appointed in January, 1832, and consisted of no less than forty-eight members, among whom were Mr. Baring, Sir James Mackintosh, Mr. Labouchere, Lord Cavendish, Mr. Villiers, Mr. O'Connell, Mr. Hume, Mr. Warburton, Viscount Morpeth, Mr. Sheil, Mr. E. Lytton Bulwer, Mr. Charles Grant, and Mr. Robert Grant. The Committee which preceded the last renewal of the Charter was appointed in November, 1852, and concluded its inquiry at the end of the session of 1853. The Committee consisted of thirty members; the late Mr. Thomas Baring was its chairman; and among those who served on the Committee were Mr. Disraeli, Lord John Russell, Mr. Gladstone, Sir James Graham, Sir W. Molesworth, Mr. Cobden, Mr. Hume, Mr. Macaulay, Lord Stanley, and Lord Palmerston. If the questions which these various Committees had to investigate were at the time considered to be so important as to make it desirable to enlist the services of the most eminent members of the House, I think it can without difficulty be shown that there are now many subjects connected with the government of India which not less urgently demand a most careful and thorough parliamentary inquiry. Although there may be much difference of opinion as to what principles should regulate the government of India, there can, I believe, be no difference of opinion that those principles, when once determined, ought to be embodied in precise and intelligible legislation. As already stated, the government of India is at the present time mainly controlled by the Act which was passed in 1858, and this Act is so obscurely worded that in attempting to interpret some of its most important provisions, the highest authorities have arrived at diametrically opposite conclusions. This will be at once seen by reference to a remarkable debate which took place in the House of Lords in 1869. In that year the Duke of Argyll, who was then Secretary of State for India, introduced a Bill which effected an important change in the tenure by which the members of the Council of the Secretary of State had hitherto held their offices. By the Act of 1858 the members of Council were to hold their offices on the same permanent tenure as an English judge. It was apparently thought that as to them was to be entrusted the duty of controlling expenditure, it was essential that their position should be made as independent as possible. Soon after the Duke of Argyll became Secretary of State it was evident that he held a different view from that which had been held by some of his predecessors, as to the functions which ought to be exercised by the Council. Considering that they were rather a consultative than a controlling body, he, with the object of securing the advice of those who had recently returned from India with fresh experience, effected a fundamental change in the tenure of the office. By the Bill to which reference has already been made the independent position of a member of Council was to a great extent weakened. He was no longer to be the holder of a permanent office, but was, in the first instance, to be appointed only for ten years, and at the end of this period he might be re-appointed by the Secretary of State for five years. As the character of the office was thus greatly changed, it almost necessarily happened that in the discussions which took place on the Bill the powers which could be exercised by the Council had to be considered. Directly, however, an attempt was made to define these powers it appeared that the highest authorities entertained entirely opposite opinions.

Thus, the Duke of Argyll, in order to bring out with distinctness the absolute divergence in the views as to the functions of the Council held by himself and by Lord Salisbury, who had recently been Secretary of State, quoted the following passage from a speech Lord Salisbury had lately made :—

"In reference to every question in which expenditure is involved—that is to say, as you well know, in reference to every question of every kind, because I believe there is hardly any question in which expenditure is not involved, directly or indirectly—the Indian Council have the power of absolute and conclusive veto by a bare majority over the decision of the Secretary of State."

Lord Salisbury, challenged to prove the accuracy of this opinion, re-affirmed it in the most positive manner, and said that he arrived at this interpretation of the Act of 1858 after consulting the very highest legal authority, who, as subsequently appeared, was Lord Cairns. On the other hand, the Duke of Argyll maintained that in arriving at exactly the opposite opinion he was supported by the Law Officers of the Crown. As the discussion proceeded this extraordinary conflict of authority became, if possible, still more marked. Lord Hatherley, who at the time was Lord Chancellor, supported the opinion that had been expressed by the Duke of Argyll as to the functions of the Council, and said Lord Cairns "appeared to give a meaning to the words of the Act which they could not bear in any sound legal construction." Commenting on these differences of opinion, Lord Salisbury maintained that it was imperatively necessary, where such vast interests were at stake, that the law should be unmistakably clear, and said that "about the doubtfulness of the law there could be no doubt whatever. When the Lord Chancellor said a thing was black, and two ex-Chancellors said it was white, there must be some doubt about the law."

A striking example of the consequences that may be produced by leaving the law in such a state of uncertainty is afforded by an event which has recently happened. Lord Salisbury and Lord Cairns, having, as has just been shown, expressed a decided opinion that "in reference to every question in which expenditure is involved . . . the Indian Council have the power of absolute and conclusive veto by a bare majority over the decision of the Secretary of State," are members of a Cabinet which adopted a "forward" frontier policy in India, involving an expenditure of millions, not only without the consent of the Council being obtained, but without the matter being brought within their cognizance.

There is apparently the same difficulty in interpreting other provisions of the Act of 1858 which are not less important than those which refer to the members of the Council of the Secretary of State. This has lately been shown in a striking manner by the controversy which arose out of the remission of the cotton duties. A majority of the members of Council of the Viceroy were opposed to the reduction of these duties, and it has been maintained on high legal authority that under these circumstances the Viceroy, in overruling the majority of his Council, put a very strained interpretation on the legal power conferred upon him. The legal member of the Council of the Viceroy may be considered the highest legal authority in India, and the present holder of that office, Mr. Whitley Stokes, referring to the course taken by the Viceroy with regard to the reduction of the Cotton Duties, used the following words:—"The proposed exemption of cotton goods, if made by a mere executive order, will thus resemble what lawyers call a fraud on the power; and there is, unfortunately, no Court of Equity to relieve the people of India against it."[1]

After what has just been stated, it cannot be necessary to multiply instances to show that the law which now regulates the Government of India is in a state of chaotic confusion. It cannot be right that there should be the widest divergence of opinion between the highest official authorities both in India and in England as to the powers which can or ought to be exercised by those who hold most influential

[1] See "Copy of Dissents recorded by Members of the Council of the Governor-General of India regarding the late Reduction of the Cotton Duties in that Country," presented to Parliament in May, 1879.

positions in the Government of India. When the Act of 1858 was passed it was intended to vest the chief financial control in the Councils of the Secretary of State and of the Viceroy. Before the abolition of the Company this control was in a great degree exercised by the Directors and by the Court of Proprietors. It invariably happened that several Directors of the East India Company were in Parliament, and the Company was thus able to exert great influence, both on English public opinion and on the English Government. If it was thought that with regard to any question in which the interests of England and India came into conflict, India was unfairly treated, the influence which was possessed by the Company both within and without the walls of Parliament was sure to be vigorously exerted on behalf of India. Under the present system, however, it is a mere matter of chance whether any one will be found in Parliament specially to watch over the interests of India. It is perfectly well known that seldom has any measure been passed which was more disliked by the people of India than the recent reduction of the cotton duties. Sir Alexander Arbuthnot, a member of the Council of the Viceroy, speaking with official responsibility, has said :—

"There can be no doubt that the people of India attribute the action which has been taken by Her

Majesty's Government in this matter to the influences which have been brought to bear upon it by persons interested in the English cotton trade, or, in other words, by the manufacturers of Lancashire."

He adds:—

"It is very undesirable that an impression should exist which, if it were well founded, would go far to justify the forebodings of those who deprecated the transfer of the direct government of India from the East India Company to the Crown on the ground that India would be sacrificed to the exigencies of political parties in Parliament. For many years after that transfer took place the propriety, and indeed the necessity, of treating Indian questions, and especially questions connected with the internal administration of India, as a thing apart from parliamentary politics, was recognised by both the great parties in the state. By a tacit but well-understood compact, India was excluded from the arena of party politics in the House of Commons. Now, for the first time, there is a prevalent belief that this understanding has been departed from. A measure seriously affecting the finances of India has been, and is being, pressed upon Parliament by a powerful section of the English mercantile community, and the general opinion is that that pressure has so far produced an effect that at a juncture of the gravest financial difficulty and anxiety the Government of India has been impelled to incur a sacrifice of revenue which the most ordinary considerations of financial prudence should have led it to retain, with the certainty that the present concession will only encourage further pressure, until the whole of the particular branch of the state revenue which has been the subject of attack shall have been abandoned."[1]

So impossible does it appear to be to interpose with any effect on behalf of India, if the wishes of her people have to be weighed against the support of a certain section of English voters, that when the action that had been taken in reference to the cotton duties was called in question in the House of Commons, the protest had to be made by a mere handful of members.

When considering in the following pages the causes which have made the present financial condition of India so unsatisfactory, numerous instances are adduced which, I believe, conclusively show that there is little hope of effecting any real and permanent improvement in her finances, unless some more adequate financial control is provided than that which is furnished by the present system of administration. As previously stated, the two bodies in whom this control was chiefly vested have, through the uncertainty of the law and other circumstances, been gradually deprived of much of the power which it was supposed they could exercise. If a Viceroy in a period of severe financial pressure can sacrifice an important branch of revenue in direct opposition to the wishes of a

[1] See Parliamentary paper just referred to.

majority of his Council; if a Secretary of State can decide upon a policy which will involve the outlay of millions, and free himself, not only from the control, but from the criticism of his Council by availing himself of the undefined powers which are vested in him of placing the despatch which orders the expenditure in the secret department—it is at once obvious that the control which these two Councils can exercise is most inadequate. Few problems in government can be more difficult than to devise the best means by which this control can be supplied. It is a problem which can only be properly solved after the most careful inquiry, which will enable due consideration to be given to the opinions of those who can speak with the greatest authority and experience. Although therefore it would now be premature to attempt to indicate the changes which should be introduced into the Government of India, no one, I think, can deny that events are every day happening which show that the reform of her administration is a matter of such urgent importance that an inquiry as to the best means of effecting it ought to be one of the first subjects to engage the attention of the new Parliament.

I.

THE FINANCIAL CONDITION OF INDIA.[1]

As there seems to be every probability that during the next few months an unusual amount of public attention will be directed to Indian affairs, I think the present may be regarded as a suitable time to consider the financial condition of that country. With the view of treating the subject with as much clearness as possible, it will be desirable in the first instance to ascertain what is the real revenue of India. Much of the complexity which so often confuses discussions on Indian finance arises from the want of any definite understanding as to the sense in which certain terms are employed. From the last financial statement of the Indian Finance Minister, it appears that he estimates the real revenue of India at between 37,000,000*l.* and 39,000,000*l.*; whereas a short time afterwards the revenue was officially stated at more than 63,000,000*l.* This great disparity of course arises from the gross revenue being referred to in the one case and the net revenue in the other. It has not unfrequently been said, in discussions on Indian

[1] February, 1879.

finance, that it cannot be of any moment whether the revenue is estimated at its gross or its net amount; it is, after all, simply a matter of account. In one sense this, no doubt, is true; but there will be no difficulty in showing that it is of the first importance to give as much prominence as possible to the net, as distinguished from the gross, revenue of India.

Few things have done so much harm to Indian finance in the past, or may cause greater embarrassment in the future, than an exaggerated idea as to the revenue which the Indian Government has to spend. Although there is much in the present financial condition of Iudia to cause serious apprehension, yet there is one circumstance connected with it which may fairly be regarded as a most hopeful omen for the future. Until quite lately, India was looked upon as an extremely wealthy country, and there was no project, however costly, that India was not supposed to be rich enough to pay for. Now, however, juster ideas of the resources of the country and of the condition of the people prevail. The recurrence of famines, and other circumstances which have caused more attention to be directed to Indian questions, have at length led the English public to take firm hold of the fact that India is an extremely poor country, and that the great mass of her people are in such a state of impoverishment that the Government will have to contend with exceptional difficulties if it becomes necessary to procure increased revenue by additional taxation. It is not more true of an individual than it is of a nation that, if it is desirable to check all extravagance, and secure rigid economy, the amount of the income which is available for expenditure should not be over-estimated. It is often said that if a man comes into possession of an encumbered estate, the mere amount of the mortgages and other debts upon the property does not form an accurate measure of the real extent of his embarrassments, for he has constantly to contend with the difficulty of possessing an income so much less than its nominal amount. Having perhaps ten thousand a year to spend, he is regarded by the world as the possessor of twice as much, and is expected every hour of his life to live accordingly. The position of India is not dissimilar to this. Year after year the Government of India has been living beyond its means. Deficits have been repeatedly recurring, and debt has been steadily and surely accumulated. Nothing, therefore, can be of greater importance, and nothing can be more likely to bring about a better state of things, than to ascertain what is the real amount of the revenue which the Indian Government has at the present time to spend.

On official authority[1] it was stated when the Indian

[1] See speech of Mr. Stanhope, the Under-Secretary of State for India, in the House of Commons, August 13, 1878. *Hansard*, vol. ccxlii.

Budget was discussed in the House of Commons, that the revenue of India in 1876–77 was 55,995,785*l*, in 1877–78 58,635,472*l*., and the revenue for 1878–79 was estimated at 63,195,000*l*. Without desiring to question the correctness of these figures as mere statements of account, I believe it can be easily proved that they are calculated to produce the most mischievous and misleading conclusions as to the true position of Indian finance. In the first place they would seem to show that the revenue of India, which is almost stationary, is rapidly increasing; and in the second place a most exaggerated opinion is likely to be formed of the resources of the Indian Government. If the items of revenue and expenditure for any year are examined, it will be at once seen that the large foregoing totals of revenue are arrived at by estimating gross instead of net revenue, and by including amongst the receipts many items which really do not represent revenue, but expenditure. Thus the following is an official statement of the ordinary revenue and expenditure for the year 1876–77.[1] In making a comparison between revenue and expenditure, I think it is fairer to select this year, because since the year 1876–77 the finances of India have been seriously disturbed by the large expenditure caused by the famine in Southern India and by the cost of the

[1] See *Finance and Revenue Accounts*, printed as a Parliamentary paper, No. 176, May 16, 1878.

Afghan war. In the following table all the items of receipt and expenditure are included which are contained in the official return. I have, however, with a view of exhibiting the accounts in the simplest possible manner, arranged the items of receipt under three classes. In the first class all those receipts are included which represent real revenue. The second class embraces those receipts which are exceeded in amount by the expenditure necessary to obtain them, and must therefore be regarded as items of expenditure rather than as sources of revenue. In the third class various items of expenditure are included, against which, as a set-off, there are no corresponding receipts.

ORDINARY REVENUE AND EXPENDITURE, 1876–77.

CLASS I. *Items of Receipt which produce Revenue.*	Gross Receipts.	Expenditure.	Net Revenue.
	£	£	£
Land	19,857,152	2,504,611	17,352,541
Opium	9,122,460	2,841,647	6,280,813
Salt	6,304,658	488,480	5,816,178
Excise on Spirits and Drugs	2,523,045	90,693	2,432,352
Customs	2,483,345	194,230	2,289,115
Stamps	2,838,628	96,266	2,742,362
Forest	598,687	436,181	162,506
Mint	258,854	130,601	128,253
Provincial contributions . .	45,894	...	45,894
Adjusting receipts from Provincial Governments (provincial deficits)	159,568		...
Adjusting receipts to Provincial Governments (provincial surpluses) . . .	...	153,726	5,842
Miscellaneous	411,335	249,622	161,713
	44,603,626	7,186,057	37,417,569
Net Revenue . .	...	...	37,417,569

	Gross Receipts.	Expenditure.	Net Revenue.
	£	£	£
Brought forward .	44,603,626	7,186,057	37,417,569
CLASS II.			
Items of receipt which, being balanced by a larger expenditure, do not represent revenue, but outlay.			
Post-Office	794,328	859,783	
Telegraph	341,227	473,127	
Gain by exchange on transactions with London . .	505,129		
Loss by exchange on transactions with London . .	...	2,181,611	
Law, Justice, and Police .	854,105	5,433,853	
Education	105,516	730,013	
Tributes and contributions .	694,934	...	
Allowances and assignments under treaties and engagements		1,672,543	
Receipts in aid of superannuation, retired, and compassionate allowances . .	607,242		
Superannuation, retired, and compassionate allowances .	...	1,798,569	
Army	925,473	15,792,112	
Marine	233,179	699,584	
Receipts for interest . . .	536,281	...	
Payment for interest on permanent and floating debt .		4,512,722	
Payment for interest on service funds, &c.	....	394,514	
Public works	198,371	3,519,668	
CLASS III.			
Items of expenditure to which there are no corresponding items of receipt.			
Administration	...	1,474,095	
Minor departments	...	320,138	
Ecclesiastical	...	163,866	
Medical	...	596,887	
Stationery and printing . .	...	443,776	
Political agencies	...	505,228	
Civil, furlough, and absentee allowances	...	235,990	
Refunds and drawbacks . .	...	291,106	
Famine relief	...	2,145,431	
TOTALS	50,399,411	51,430,673	37,417,569

From these figures certain conclusions can be drawn, which may be regarded as of fundamental importance in forming a correct opinion as to the actual position of Indian finance. It thus appears, and it is a fact which cannot be kept too prominently in view, that the entire revenue of India, with the exception of 504,208*l.*, is derived from the six following sources: land, opium, salt, excise, customs, and stamps. The various other items of revenue mentioned in the accounts cannot be fairly considered as sources of revenue. They do not in fact produce revenue; but, on the contrary, should be regarded as causes of expenditure. Thus the revenue of 794,328*l.* from the Post Office requires an expenditure of 859,783*l.* to obtain it. A receipt of 341,227*l.* from the telegraph is more than balanced by an expenditure of 473,127*l.* But if any further illustration were needed to show that no accurate idea can be formed of the real revenue of India by adding together all the items of receipt which are now included in the statement annually published of revenue and expenditure, it is only necessary to refer to the items of receipt which have been arranged under Class II. Amongst these there is one of 505,129*l.* described as "gain by exchange." When it is remembered that in this very year India had to bear a most serious loss from exchange, amounting to no less than 2,181,611*l.*, it is evident that, if any good could result from augmenting her nominal revenue, 2,000,000*l.* might be added to each side of the account, and the gain by exchange might be represented as 2,500,000*l.*[1] But unless the subject is confused by unnecessary complications, nothing can be more easy than to arrive at correct conclusions with regard to the amount of the real revenue of India. It has been already stated that the revenue, with the exception of the sum of 504,208*l.*, is derived from land, opium, salt, excise, customs, and stamps, and if, as has been done in the above table, the cost of collecting each of these items of revenue is deducted from their gross amount, the real revenue of India is shown to be only 37,417,569*l.* The conclusion which has been just arrived at as to the amount of

[1] It is sometimes said that no harm can result from exhibiting the Indian revenue at its gross instead of its net amount, because the same course is adopted with regard to the English revenue and expenditure. There is, however, such a fundamental difference between the position of English and Indian finance, that a mode of exhibiting revenue which may be perfectly suited to the one country is altogether unsuited to the other. Thus the difference between the gross and net revenue of England is much smaller than the difference between the gross and net revenue of India. In 1877 the gross revenue of England was 78,565,036*l.*, and its net revenue was not less than 68,000,000*l.* Many of the items of receipt which in India are balanced by a larger corresponding expenditure represent in England important sources of revenue. Thus, the Post Office, as has been shown, causes to India a loss of about 65,000*l.*, while it yields in England a net revenue of more than 2,000,000*l.*, after allowing for the cost of the packet service.

the real revenue of India is fully confirmed by the Indian Finance Minister, Sir John Strachey, who, about twelve months since, estimated the net ordinary expenditure of India at between 37,000,000*l.* and 38,000,000*l.*, and said that the ordinary revenue is only just sufficient to meet it.

It may perhaps be thought that I have laid too much stress on the importance of keeping steadily in view the distinction between the gross and net revenue of India; but it can scarcely be denied that, if excessive expenditure is bringing embarrassment upon the finances of a country, nothing is more essential to secure strict economy than, as far as possible, to discourage any exaggerated estimate being formed of the actual amount of such a country's revenue. Thus, as one illustration, it may be mentioned that the military expenditure of India is estimated by Sir John Strachey at more than 17,000,000*l.* a year. Such an expenditure would be sufficiently serious if it were defrayed out of a revenue which was, as the Indian revenue has been represented to be, rapidly increasing from 56,000,000*l.* to 63,000,000*l.*; but how incalculably more serious must such an expenditure be, and how much more likely is it that retrenchment will be demanded as an imperative necessity, when it appears that this enormous charge of more than 17,000,000*l.* a year has to be met, not out of an increasing revenue of 63,000,000*l.*, but out of an almost stationary revenue of about 38,000,000*l.*

In the statement that has been given of the receipts and expenditure for the year 1876-1877, it was shown that the ordinary revenue fell short of the ordinary expenditure by about 1,000,000*l.* As it may be thought that this year was an exceptional one, it will be desirable again to refer to the financial statement of Sir J. Strachey; for nothing can be more explicit than the opinion he expresses that the normal condition of Indian finance is one in which the ordinary revenue is barely sufficient to meet the ordinary expenditure. Thus he says :—

"A careful examination of the accounts of the seven years ending on the 31st of March, 1876, a period long enough to illustrate fairly the state of our finances, made it plain not only that we had, when I spoke, made no proper provision for the cost of famines, but that we possessed no true surplus of revenue over expenditure to cover the many contingencies to which a great country is exposed."[1]

Of the many contingencies necessitating increased expenditure to which Sir John Strachey refers, it is

[1] See speech of Sir John Strachey in bringing forward his proposals for the creation of a Famine Fund. Calcutta, December 28, 1877. This speech, which contains a most able review of the finances of India, was published in the session of 1878 as a Parliamentary paper.

only necessary here to mention two—War and Famine. At the time he spoke India was in a state of profound peace; but within less than a twelvemonth a war has been undertaken which will throw upon her finances a charge, the amount of which it is impossible at the present time to calculate. For the other contingency famine, Sir John Strachey was at the time attempting to make some provision by imposing additional taxation on the people of India. In view of the occurrence within twelve years of four serious famines in different parts of India, and of the fact that between 1873 and 1878 famines have thrown a charge upon the Indian revenues of no less than 16,000,000*l.*, no other alternative presents itself to the Indian Government than to treat famines, not as exceptional or accidental occurrences, but as calamities which are so certain to recur that provision should be made to meet them out of the ordinary revenue of the year. The amount that is required to provide an adequate fund for the relief of famines was estimated at 1,500,000*l.* a year. As the Government of India have repeatedly declared that they are fully sensible of the very serious consequences, both financial and political, that may be produced by adding to the taxation of India, it cannot be supposed that they would sanction additional taxation unless they were compelled to do so by urgent necessity. Nothing, therefore, can more conclusively show that the ordinary revenue of India is only just sufficient to meet its ordinary expenditure, no margin being left to provide for those many contingencies which it is officially stated are certain to recur, than the fact that a careful financier like Sir John Strachey admitted that, in order to create the Famine Fund which he says is essential to place the finances of India on a sound basis, no other course was open to him than to provide this fund from new taxation. I shall subsequently have occasion to describe the particular taxes which have been imposed with the object of creating this fund; and fully admitting that the Indian Government would not wantonly or unnecessarily impose taxation which is exceptionally unjust and burdensome, nothing can more forcibly illustrate the gravity of the financial position of India at the present time than the circumstance that, amongst the new taxes which have recently been imposed, it has been thought requisite to levy what is virtually an income-tax of fivepence in the pound on incomes of no more than four shillings a week. But, before considering the nature of the new taxation that has lately been imposed in India, and before showing to what straits the Indian Government will be reduced if in future years they should have to obtain additional revenue to meet recurring deficits, it will be desirable to make as careful an estimate as possible of the future prospects of the revenue and expenditure of that country.

It must be evident that no question relating to Indian finance can be of more fundamental importance than to examine the chief items of her revenue and expenditure, with the object of ascertaining whether, if expenditure increases, it is likely to be met by a corresponding growth of revenue. If such an examination is made, I am afraid that no other conclusion can be arrived at, than that the outlook for the future is gloomy in the extreme. It will be shown that if India continues to be governed as she now is, and if no change is introduced into the administration of her finances, it is inevitable that any possible growth of her revenue will be altogether inadequate to meet the certain increase in her expenditure, and no other prospect will lie before her Government but augmented indebtedness and additional taxation.

Reverting to the six sources from which the revenue of India is derived—namely, land, opium, salt, excise, customs, and stamps—I will, as briefly as possible, consider what is the probability of an increase in each separate head of revenue. With regard to the land revenue, from which nearly one-half of the entire net revenue of India is obtained, it is scarcely necessary to remark that there cannot, from the manner in which the land revenue has been settled, be any material increase in its amount for a considerable number of years. Over a large portion of the most fertile districts of India, the land revenue is permanently settled; the Government having commuted the land revenue for a fixed annual rent-charge to be paid in silver. Of the entire land revenue about one-fifth is derived from the permanently settled districts, and therefore, as far as this portion is concerned, it is incapable of any augmentation. In the North-West Provinces, and in other parts of India, what are known as thirty years' settlements prevail. The amount of the land revenue, in these districts, is fixed for thirty years, and until the expiration of this period it is of course impossible that there can be any increased assessment. From time to time, as these thirty years' settlements fall in, the land can be reassessed; but many who are most competent to express an opinion confidently assert that the agricultural classes in India, except in the pemanently settled districts, where an increase of the land revenue cannot be obtained, are not in a condition to bear a heavier assessment.

Although there would thus appear to be no immediate probability of the amount derived from the land revenue being materially increased, there is unfortunately no room whatever for doubt that the real value of this revenue has been within the last few years most seriously lessened. The land revenue is really a rent paid to the Indian Government in silver, and the amount of this silver rent is fixed, either permanently or for a defined period. A very considerable part of the expenditure of the Indian Government consists of payments which have to be made in gold. At least 17,000,000*l.*, or about 45 per cent. of the entire net revenue of India, is expended in England in paying the interest on the Indian debt, in the purchase of stores, in salaries, pensions, &c., and this large and increasing outlay, known as the home charges, has to be made in gold. The Indian Government receives its revenue in silver, but has to find gold for the purpose of defraying 45 per cent. of its expenditure. Within the last few years there has been a most serious depreciation in the value of silver when compared with gold. Silver has fallen from 60*d.* to about 50*d.* an ounce; a sovereign, which could formerly be purchased with four ounces of silver, can now only be purchased with five ounces. Consequently about 20 per cent. more silver is now required to pay the home charges than would be needed if there were no depreciation in the value of silver. The net land revenue is about equivalent in amount to the net home charges, and consequently, if this revenue were appropriated to defray these charges, it would virtually be reduced in value at least 3,000,000*l.* a year, owing to the depreciation in the value of silver. With regard, therefore, to the future prospects of the land revenue, I think it may be concluded, first, that there is little probability of any immediate increase in its amount, and secondly, that the depreciation of silver seriously lessens the real value of this revenue.

Next proceeding to consider the revenue derived from opium, there is no branch of Indian revenue which has lately shown so large an increase. It appears from an official paper which was laid before Parliament as recently as December, 1878, that the revenue from opium during the current financial year is likely to exceed the estimate by no less a sum than 1,240,000*l.* It has been stated that a part of this large increase is due to the Government, pressed by the necessity of finding funds for the Afghan war, having brought an unusually large quantity of opium into the market. But, whether this be so or not, I think it cannot be denied that no inconsiderable part of this increase in the revenue from opium must be due to a rise in the price of opium produced by the depreciation in the value of silver. For some time after the fall in the price of silver took place there appeared to be no movement in general prices in

India. Silver, in fact, had simply fallen in value in relation to gold. Now, however, there seems to be a depreciation in the general value of silver in India, and prices are beginning to rise; for in the same official return in which an estimate is given of the large increase of revenue expected to be derived from opium, it is stated that on account of a rise in the price of food, the army expenditure in India is estimated during the present financial year to exceed the estimate by 330,000*l.* As the Indian Government sells opium in the open market, the amount of the opium revenue will, in the absence of any counteracting circumstances, increase with the rise in general prices. Although, therefore, there is this favourable circumstance connected with the opium revenue, namely, that it is not prejudicially affected in the same way as the land revenue must be, by the depreciation in the value of silver, yet no prudent financier should ignore the fact that this revenue depends almost for its existence upon the action of the Chinese Government in admitting Indian opium to their ports, while they forbid the cultivation of opium in China. Much valuable information on the subject of the opium revenue is contained in the evidence given before the Parliamentary Committee on Indian Finance. Among the many witnesses who were examined on this question there is no one whose opinion is entitled to more consideration than Sir Rutherford Alcock, who had not only resided in China for twenty-five years, but who at the time was her Majesty's Minister in that country. In the evidence he gave before the Select Committee on Indian Finance (May 23, 1871), he expressed the opinion that the Chinese Government were seriously contemplating putting an end to the importation of opium, and allowing its cultivation without stint in China. I do not presume to express any opinion of my own on the extent to which the opium revenue is likely to be affected by any action that may be taken by the Government of China. My sole object in calling attention to the subject is to show that the most productive of all the sources of Indian revenue, next to land, may, in the opinion of some most competent judges, be seriously reduced in consequence of a falling off in the Chinese demand for Indian opium; and it therefore becomes the more essential that the finances of India should be administered with the utmost care and thrift.

Next proceeding to consider the prospect of an increased revenue being obtained from salt, it will, I think, be admitted that, although a small increase of revenue may be derived from an increase of population, yet nothing could justify an attempt to obtain an additional revenue from salt by raising the rate of the existing duties. The duty now imposed, amounting to no less than 2,000 per cent. on the prime cost of the article, cannot but be regarded as a most onerous impost, when it is remembered that salt is as much a necessary of life as the air we breathe or the water we drink. It seems, moreover, that taxation on salt has reached that point when it produces a most serious effect in checking consumption. This is particularly the case in the poorest parts of India, such as Madras. This was felt so strongly by the late Lord Hobart, the able Governor of that Presidency, that he declared that nothing would induce him to be a consenting party to an increase of the salt duty. At the time Lord Hobart made that declaration, the duty levied on salt in Madras was one rupee, thirteen annas per maund. Within the last twelvemonth, the salt duty has been raised in Madras and Bombay from one rupee, thirteen annas to two rupees, eight annas. This increase of nearly 40 per cent. in the duty, has been defended as a part of a scheme for the equalisation of the salt duties throughout India. If, however, the equalisation of duties is an object of so much importance as to justify a large addition to the duty being imposed on the people of Madras and Bombay at the very moment when they were recovering from the ravages of a terrible famine, it at once becomes evident that the duties cannot be raised in India without departing from this policy of equalisation; for I believe it will be admitted that nothing could justify the raising of the salt duty in Madras and Bombay beyond the point to which it has recently been advanced.

With regard to the last three branches of revenue —excise, customs, and stamps—little need be said. The present aggregate net revenue obtained from customs and excise does not amount to more than 5,000,000*l.* a year; and the policy of the Government in recent years has been rather to diminish than to increase these duties. Moreover, one of the most important items in the receipt from customs, namely, that derived from the import duty now imposed on cotton goods, must be regarded as existing on a somewhat precarious tenure. The repeal of this duty has been earnestly demanded by the cotton-manufacturing interest in England; and the Government entered into an undertaking that the duty should be repealed as soon as the financial condition of India permitted. It is somewhat difficult to define the exact interpretation to be given to this promise; but it is evident that its fulfilment will be persistently, and possibly successfully, urged. For when it was recently affirmed on the authority of the Secretary of State that India possessed a balance from which the expenses of the Afghan war could be defrayed, it was immediately said by the manufacturing interest in Lancashire that if such a balance really existed its appropriation had been beforehand pledged to the repeal of the import duty on cotton goods. As, therefore, this important item of receipt in the customs duties of India will be liable to constant attack from persons possessing great power and political influence in England, and as there is no new excise duty which it has been suggested could be imposed, I think no other conclusion can be arrived at than that not only is there little chance of obtaining additional revenue from customs and excise, but, on the contrary, the Indian Government may, in face of the promises they have made about the cotton duties, find it difficult to maintain the revenue which they now receive.

In reference to stamps, it is only necessary to remark that if it were practicable to obtain additional revenue from this source, stamps would certainly not have escaped the watchful eye of the Indian financiers, who, when last year they were creating a famine fund, were apparently so hard pressed that, as previously stated, they were compelled to subject to direct taxation incomes of only four shillings a week.

This brief review of the general prospect of the Indian revenue is, I think, sufficient to show not only that this revenue is comparatively stationary in amount, but that as the revenue is received in silver, and a large part of it has to be devoted to making payments in gold, the real value of this revenue has been, and may continue to be, most seriously diminished by the depreciation of silver. This conclusion as to the inelasticity of the Indian revenue is strongly confirmed by the extremely slow growth of the revenue during the past ten years, from 1868 to 1877. This particular period is selected for comparison because the figures are to be found in the latest number which has been published of the *Statistical Abstract of British India.* It appears from the table already given that four-fifths of the entire net revenue of India is derived from land, opium, and salt; and the inelastic character of the Indian revenue is at once shown if the average yield of these three sources of revenue, from 1868 to 1872, is compared with their average yield from 1873 to 1877.

	Average during five years, from 1868 to 1872.	Average during five years, from 1873 to 1877.
	£	£
Net Land Revenue . . .	17,991,951	18,526,451
Net Opium ,, ...	6,720,672	6,388,555
Net Salt ,, ...	5,466,370	5,735,936
TOTALS	30,178,993	30,650,942

It will be extremely important to keep these conclusions as to the inelasticity of the Indian revenue steadily in mind when considering, as I now propose to do, the prospects of Indian expenditure. It will not be necessary to examine all the detailed items of this expenditure, for I believe it will be perfectly possible to obtain data from which a correct opinion on the subject can be formed, by directing attention to the four chief branches of expenditure—namely, military expenditure, cost of administration, loss by exchange, and interest on loans for the general purposes of government, as well as for public works.

No subject connected with Indian finance demands such prompt and anxious attention as the enormous and increasing burden which is thrown upon India by her military expenditure. I have already referred to the fact that, even in a time of peace, the cost of the army to India is upwards of 17,000,000*l.* a year, 45 per cent. of her entire net revenue of 37,500,000*l.* being thus absorbed. It seems moreover that no limit can be placed to the extent to which India may not be exhausted by this drain on her resources. In the financial statement of 1878, allusion was made to the significant fact that the cost of the army being at that time more than 17,000,000*l.*, had increased by "upwards of

1,000,000*l.* since 1875–76, and that a large part of this increase was in the expenditure recorded in the home accounts." But serious as seemed to be the danger, at the time when these words were spoken, that India was gradually having thrown upon her a military expenditure which with her stationary revenue she would be absolutely powerless to bear, yet how indefinitely has this danger been increased by the events of the last few months. I shall carefully abstain from saying a single word on the Afghan war which is not most strictly relevant to the subject now under discussion. It is, however, of the utmost importance to the future of India that the consequences involved in carrying out what is known as a "forward" frontier policy should be considered in their financial as well as in their military aspects. It would not be more unreasonable to decide what is the best house for a particular individual to live in, without having any regard to his income, than it is, on a mere consideration of military tactics, to determine to advance the frontier of India, without first ascertaining the expenditure which such an advance would necessitate. It is particularly worthy of remark that those who have been foremost in advocating a "forward" frontier policy in India have apparently ignored any consideration of its cost. The long and able statements of Sir Henry Rawlinson, Sir Bartle Frere, and Lord Napier of Magdala, contain scarcely a single reference to the financial aspects of the policy which they advocate. On the other hand, nothing can be more precise than the declarations of many of those most competent to express an opinion on the question, that the frontier could not be advanced without causing a most serious permanent addition to the military expenditure of India. Lord Lawrence, speaking of such an advance as is now contemplated, declared that it would "paralyse the finances of India." This was not simply his individual opinion. It has been often said that no Governor-General was ever surrounded by abler men than those who constituted the Council of the Viceroy in 1867, and the despatch which contains this remarkable declaration was signed not only by Lord Lawrence, but by the Commander-in-Chief, Sir W. H. Mansfield (afterwards Lord Sandhurst), Sir H. S. Maine, Mr. G. N. Taylor, Mr. W. N. Massey, Sir Henry Durand, and Mr. G. U. Yule. This despatch, moreover, was addressed to Sir Stafford Northcote, who was then Secretary of State for India, and its conclusions were accepted by him and the Government of which he was a member. In view of these facts I think it may be fairly asked, if the expenditure necessary to carry out a particular policy would have paralysed the finances of India in 1867, what single circumstance can be pointed to which would show that such an expenditure would produce less serious consequences at the present time? No one can pretend to say that India's financial condition is more flourishing now than it was then. Since 1867 she has had to bear the severe strain of successive famines; and in 1867 there seemed to be no probability that her finances would be crippled by that depreciation of silver which has been said by one who spoke with the authority of a Finance Minister "to cast a grave shadow on the future of Indian finance."[1] In case it may be objected that these opinions of Lord Lawrence and his Council were expressed before the publication of the memorandum of Sir Henry Rawlinson, who throughout has been the most influential advocate of a "forward" policy, it may be well to point out that after this memorandum had been submitted to all the highest authorities in India, there is not a single word to be found in any of the minutes which they wrote upon it, which can be interpreted as the expression of a more favourable opinion of the financial results which would be produced by advancing the frontier into Afghanistan. Thus Sir R. H. Davies, the Lieutenant-Governor of the Punjaub, says: "Sir H. Rawlinson's

[1] See speech of Sir W. Muir at Calcutta, April 10, 1876.

proposals would again plunge us into the ever-shifting sands of Central Asian intrigue at a cost which we cannot afford." Sir Richard Temple, who has filled many influential positions in India, says: "Under Providence we are trustees for the public funds of India, and we are responsible for the careful application of them. When there are so many objects of certain usefulness and necessity within India itself on which to spend this money, it is a grave thing to expend such money in foreign regions on objects of doubtful expediency."[1] The very evil which Sir R. Temple thus anticipated has actually come to pass; for as Governor of Bombay he has himself been obliged, under the financial pressure caused by the military expenditure in Afghanistan, to peremptorily order that all public works, nay, even all repairs except those which are absolutely necessary, should be stopped in that Presidency.

In order to obtain as distinct an idea as possible of the consequences which may be produced on the financial condition of India by carrying out this "forward" frontier policy, it will be desirable to refer to some estimates which have been made of its cost by those most competent to form an opinion. The late Lord Sandhurst, who was scarcely less distinguished as a financier than as a soldier, writing in

[1] See Afghan Papers, 1878.

1875, declared that the occupation of the advanced positions which it is proposed should be held beyond our present frontier, would require an addition to the strength both of the European and native army in India which would permanently increase her military expenditure by more than 3,000,000*l.* a year. One of the very highest of Indian military authorities, Sir Henry Norman, has lately declared that if the advance were confined simply to the occupation of Koorrum, Jellalabad or Daka, and Candahar, at least thirteen or fourteen thousand additional troops would be required, one-third of whom would have to be British, and that their cost would be 1,000,000*l.* per annum ; this sum, moreover, is independent of the large amount that would have to be expended on fortifications and other military works, and also in subsidising the hill tribes. It is, however, scarcely necessary to refer even to such high authorities as those just quoted. It can no longer be regarded as a matter of surmise that the frontier policy, which is now being pursued in India, will make a most serious permanent addition to her military expenditure. Less than a month had elapsed from the time our troops had crossed the frontier when it was announced that it had been decided to increase the native army by 15,000 men, or about 12 per cent. There is no point connected with the government of India on which there is greater unanimity of opinion than that it would not be prudent to add to the number of the native army without proportionately increasing the strength of the European army. An increase of 12 per cent. in the European and native army will certainly involve a cost of not less than 1,500,000*l.* a year. It would therefore appear that two powerful agencies will be brought simultaneously into operation most seriously to augment the military expenditure of India. In the first place, as Sir John Strachey has pointed out, the army, from administrative causes, is becoming more costly in proportion to its numbers; and, in the second place, the policy which is now being pursued is necessitating a very material addition to the strength of the army. The extremely grave consequences involved in such an increase of military expenditure will be shown when considering whether, in the present financial condition of India, there is any probability that such new charges can be met, without imposing taxes intolerably burdensome to the people, or accumulating an indebtedness which will augment the taxation that will ultimately have to be imposed.

Passing on to consider the second of the four chief branches of expenditure—namely, the general cost of administration—the evidence which was given before the Parliamentary Committee on Indian Finance affords almost innumerable examples of the striking manner in which the various items which compose this general cost of administration have increased during the last twenty years. A most valuable table was furnished to the Committee by Mr. Gay, the Deputy Comptroller-General of the Finances, in which a comparison is made between the cost of administration in 1871 and 1856, two years before the abolition of the East India Company. From this table it appears that the cost of the government of India, excluding expenditure on the army and public works, has increased during the period referred to from 14,964,867*l.* to 23,271,082*l.*[1] There is scarcely a single item in which there has not been a marked augmentation, and this growth has continued up to the present time. Thus, taking a few instances:—

	1856-57.	1870-71.
	£	£
Superannuation, retired, and compassionate allowances	424,930	655,969
Stationery and printing	128,197	233,675
Medical services	175,714	523,486

I believe it can be shown that a part at least of the large increase in the general cost of administration is undoubtedly due to a want of adequate economy; but without, for the moment, inquiring what portion of this increase of expenditure could have been

[1] See Appendix to Report of Committee on East Indian Finance, 1872, p. 518.

prevented if India, since the abolition of the East India Company, had been governed with less extravagance, it is obvious that the greater the extent to which this additional outlay has arisen from causes the operation of which cannot be controlled, the more serious is the prospect for the future. If money has been wasted in the past, the continuance of this waste can be prevented; but a remedy cannot be so easily applied if the cost of a particular department becomes greater in consequence, for instance, of a rise in prices. The very detailed evidence which was given before the Indian Finance Committee by Mr. Harrison, Comptroller-General of India, leaves no room for doubt that a not inconsiderable portion of the increase in the cost of administration between 1856 and 1871 was due to a rise in general prices. There was during this period, and especially at the time of the American Civil War, a very large influx of silver into India. A portion of this silver was sent to purchase cotton at extremely high prices; and another portion represented capital which was raised in England and sent to India for the construction of railways and other works. At the present time there seem to be indications that the financial position of India may be prejudicially affected by a rise in general prices consequent on a depreciation in the value of silver. Allusion has already been made to the fact that as recently as December, 1878, an official paper was published from which it appears that the military expenditure of the present year will be greater than its estimated amount by 330,000*l.*, which is described as "compensation for high price of food." It is evident that if there is a rise in general prices there is scarcely a single department, the cost of which may not, sooner or later, very materially increase. It is not, however, necessary here to pursue the subject further, because the extent to which general prices in India may be affected by the depreciation of silver can be more appropriately considered when discussing the third of the four branches of expenditure—namely, that which arises from loss by exchange.

In the current financial year the loss by exchange was estimated, when the budget was brought forward, at no less than 3,000,000*l.*; but, large as this sum is, the Government, in a revised estimate issued within the last few weeks, calculate that it will be exceeded by 500,000*l.* In 1876-7 the loss by exchange, as appears from the table already given, was 1,676,482*l.* In 1874-75 the loss by exchange was only about 500,000*l.* A few years previous to this the loss was so trifling as scarcely to be worth notice; and in 1870 the amount which was gained by exchange exceeded, by a few thousand pounds, the amount lost. These figures show, with striking distinctness, with what remarkable rapidity this item in Indian expenditure has assumed its present serious proportions. Whether it is more likely that this charge on the Indian revenues will in future years diminish or increase, depends upon so many uncertain conditions that it would not be prudent to make a confident prediction on the subject. The loss by exchange, as previously explained, is primarily due to a depreciation in the value of silver, and one of the chief causes of this depreciation is the large additional supply of silver yielded by the Nevada mines in recent years. In 1875 the aggregate production of silver throughout the world is estimated to have been about 15,000,000*l*., more than half of this amount, 8,000,000*l*. being obtained from the American mines. Twenty years previously—namely, between 1852 and 1862—the average annual production was only from 8,000,000*l*. to 9,000,000*l*., and at that time no appreciable quantity came from the United States. Simultaneously with this large increase in the supply of silver many circumstances occurred which greatly diminished the demand for silver. Silver was demonetised in Germany; and Germany consequently not only ceased to require the large amount of silver which she had previously used for coinage, but a great portion of the silver in circulation was withdrawn and sold by the German

Government. Another circumstance which has produced a very important effect in diminishing the demand for silver is the great increase in recent years in the Indian home charges. The value of the products exported from India has always been much in excess of the value of those imported. Until quite lately the balance was liquidated by transmitting silver to India. In some years the silver thus sent amounted to more than 10,000,000*l*. Such a transmission of silver constituted one of the chief sources of the demand for silver, and was indeed one of the most important factors in maintaining its value. Each addition, however, that is made to the home charges diminishes *pro tanto* this demand for silver. An English merchant, for instance, who has purchased a hundred thousand pounds' worth of Indian produce, instead of sending silver to India to pay for it, purchases bills from the Indian Government in England, drawn upon the Indian Government in Calcutta, and the amount of bills which the Government has to sell in England increases, of course, with each increase in the home charges. It is, I think, made sufficiently clear from this brief review of the various circumstances which have produced a depreciation in the value of silver, and a consequent loss by exchange to the Indian Government, that the value of silver depends upon various causes, some of which may be regarded as entirely beyond the power of any Government to control. Thus the value of silver will be to a very considerable extent determined by the future yield of the American mines. It is impossible to foresee whether the future productiveness of these mines will increase or diminish, and it may of course happen that silver mines may be discovered in other parts of the world. It has, however, been shown that a powerful effect is being exerted at the present time in depreciating the value of silver by the large amount of bills which have to be sold by the Indian Government in England to provide for the home charges. The amount of the home charges has increased to a most serious extent in recent years. Nothing, moreover, can avert a still further increase, if the expenditure is permitted so habitually to exceed the revenue that money has to be borrowed to make good the deficit. The loans being chiefly raised in England, it is obvious that the interest on these loans represents so much more which has to be transmitted from India to England, or, in other words, so much added to the home charges.

It is important to direct particular attention to the influence exerted by each increase in the home charges in adding to the loss by exchange which India has to bear, since under any circumstances it would be a cause for apprehension to see a constantly augmenting proportion of the revenue of a country not spent in the country itself; but this circumstance becomes more serious when it can be shown that this expenditure of the revenues of India out of India exerts a direct influence in depreciating the value of silver, and in thus lessening the value of all that large part of the Indian revenue which, either permanently or temporarily, is received in the form of a fixed payment made in silver.

With regard to the fourth and last branch of expenditure to which I have called attention—namely, the interest on loans—it is manifest that this subject is closely connected in many of its aspects with the question which has just been considered. The largest portion of the money which has been borrowed in recent years by the Indian Government has been obtained by loans raised in England; and the additional amount which has to be provided to meet the interest on these loans represents so much added to the home charges. In 1856 the sum annually required to pay the interest on the Indian Debt was 2,190,000*l.*, in 1870-71 it was 3,200,000*l.*, and in 1876-77 it was 4,350,000*l.* From these figures it appears that in twenty years the annual charge for interest on the Indian Debt increased by about 100 per cent. Nothing can be more certain than that, in the present financial condition of India, this indebtedness must continue steadily to increase. The figures which have already been quoted, conclusively show that the ordinary revenue of India is only barely sufficient to meet the ordinary expenditure, and that consequently, in the words of one who speaks with official authority, every fresh contingency and every new charge involve some addition to the debt of India. Thus, within the last few years, 16,000,000*l.* has been spent in famine relief, and nearly the whole of this amount has been obtained by loans, the interest on which involves an annual charge of about 700,000*l.* Money, however, is not borrowed by the Indian Government simply to meet such charges as these; it has for some time been their settled policy to borrow each year not less than 4,000,000*l.* for the construction of railways and works of irrigation. The public works, which are thus constructed out of borrowed money, are no doubt undertaken by the Indian Government with the idea that they will be reproductive, or, in other words, that they will yield a net revenue sufficient to pay the interest on the capital expended. The experience of the past, however, proves that, although it is intended that these public works should be reproductive in the sense just described, yet, regarding the transaction simply as a financial one, the money thus spent is really embarked in a most speculative and uncertain investment. Lord Salisbury, speaking at Manchester in January 1875, when he was Secretary of State for India, said :—

"The difficulties which surround the question of irrigation are very great. We can scarcely yet be said to have had one genuine instance of financial success. The irrigating projects that have been carried out, if they have had for their basis the former works of native rulers, have in many instances been a financial success; but then of course that favourable appearance of the account has been obtained by not charging the former expenditure of the native ruler. In those cases where we have begun the projects of irrigation for ourselves we have not reached, I believe, in any one instance, the desired result of a clean balance-sheet."

Although I think that Lord Salisbury, in making this sweeping assertion about the unsatisfactory financial results of these irrigation works, somewhat overstated the case, yet it is impossible for any one to deny the absolute correctness of the conclusion which has been officially arrived at, that on the 9,000,000*l.* which has been spent in recent years on schemes of irrigation in Bengal, the return which is yielded is only ½ per cent.[1] When it is remembered

[1] See Speech of Lord G. Hamilton, when Under-Secretary of State for India, in the House of Commons, January, 1878. *Hansard*, vol. ccxxxvii. p. 331.

that every one of these particular works, at the time it was undertaken, was regarded as reproductive, nothing more need be said to show that, however useful or desirable public works may be in India, it is more than probable that they will not yield a return sufficient to meet the interest on the capital expended; and consequently there will be a deficit which will represent another item of expenditure, another charge upon the revenues of India. It therefore appears that at the present time the indebtedness of India must almost inevitably continue to be augmented by two distinct causes. In the first place, as there is no surplus of ordinary revenue beyond ordinary expenditure, every such contingency as war or famine is certain to lead to the debt being increased; and, secondly, so long as the present policy is continued of constructing public works out of borrowed money, the loans which are raised for these works represent constant additions to the debt of India.

Many other branches of Indian expenditure might be referred to, besides those to which attention has been here directed. I think, however, enough has been said on the subject of revenue and expenditure to establish the following conclusions with regard to the financial position of India:—

1. The revenue is characterised by great inelasticity.

2. The expenditure has increased in a marked manner in recent years, partly from the general increase in the cost of administration, and partly from a depreciation in the value of silver.

3. The military expenditure is excessive, absorbing 45 per cent. of the entire net revenue of the country; and this expenditure is likely to be greatly augmented if the frontier of India is advanced, as now seems to be contemplated.

4. A comparatively stationary revenue having to meet an increasing expenditure, it will be necessary sooner or later to add to the taxation of India. If a deficit is temporarily met by borrowing, the money which will have to be provided to pay the interest on the loan must ultimately increase the deficit, which will have to be met by increased taxation.

5. There has already been a most serious increase in the indebtedness of India, amounting in twenty years to 100 per cent.

Such being the present condition of Indian finance, scarcely another word need be said to show that if some fundamental change is not promptly introduced, if expenditure is not rigorously curtailed, it will be absolutely impossible to avoid the necessity of imposing on the people of India a large amount of additional taxation. In order adequately to appreciate the grave consequences which may be produced by an increase of taxation in India, it is essential to bear in mind that the question cannot be regarded as if it were simply a financial one. Between England and India, in matters of taxation, there is a fundamental difference. If some contingency should occur in England which would render it necessary to obtain 5,000,000*l.* by additional taxation, it is perfectly well known how easily the money could be provided. More than 5,000,000*l.* could be raised by adding twopence in the pound to the income-tax, and by slightly increasing the duty on some article of general consumption, such as tea or spirits. But in India, if it became necessary to raise, not 5,000,000*l.*, but even a smaller sum, say 3,000,000*l.*, by additional taxation, it will scarcely be denied that taxes might have to be imposed which would be regarded by the people as so burdensome as to create a most serious amount of discontent. When examining in detail the present sources of revenue, I believe it was clearly proved that they present so little prospect of increase that, if additional revenue has to be obtained, it will be absolutely necessary to have recourse to some new forms of taxation. The truth of this conclusion is corroborated in a most striking manner by the recent action of the Indian Government. In order to obtain the comparatively trifling sum of 750,000*l.*, the Government came to the conclusion, as already stated, that no better course was open to them than to impose a trades licence tax of fivepence in the pound upon all trade incomes, even on those as small as 4*s.* a week. As the Government of India must have been fully aware of the discontent which such a tax would inevitably cause, it may be fairly concluded that they would never have sanctioned it, if they could have discovered any less unsatisfactory way of obtaining the money required. But if the trades licence tax was regarded, a twelvemonth since, as the best mode of obtaining additional revenue, one of two things must occur if it becomes necessary still further to add to taxation in order to provide for the increasing expenditure which is now taking place—either the rate of the licence tax must be advanced, or some tax which the Government considered, a twelvemonth since, still more objectionable must be resorted to. It is already rumoured that the income-tax will again be imposed; and although this tax has often been supported on the ground that it will reach a wealthy class who are least heavily taxed, yet nothing can be more unwise than to ignore the very serious disadvantages associated with the levying of such a tax in India. It was unequivocally condemned by three successive Indian Finance Ministers. The practical objections to the tax, as distinguished from the theoretical arguments that may be adduced in its favour, have been stated with remarkable clearness by Mr. Laing, who for many years served in India as Finance Minister. He has said that he regarded the income-tax as "about as bad and obnoxious a mode of raising revenue as it is possible to imagine in a country like India .... I think that for an Oriental country, and with the Eastern habit of mind, any tax which imposes inquisition into individual means is attended with innumerable evils which are little felt in a country like England." And he further expressed an opinion that, in consequence of the impossibility of preventing abuses connected with the assessment of the tax in a country like India, "for every rupee that comes into the Treasury, two rupees are extorted from the population that have to pay the tax."

Probably, however, one of the most weighty objections that can be urged against the imposition of an income-tax in India is that a great machinery of assessment, which it has been shown is liable to the gravest abuse, is brought into active operation over the length and breadth of the country, in order to realise a very trifling financial result. When this tax was last levied in India, it was at the rate of twopence-halfpenny in the pound, and the net revenue realised was little more than 500,000*l*. From an income-tax of twopence-halfpenny in the pound in

England about 5,000,000*l.* would be obtained, and many small incomes which would be exempted in England would certainly be assessed in India. No fact can bring out with more striking distinctness the remarkable contrast between the wealth of England and the poverty of India. India contains a population more than seven times as great as that of England, and yet a tax which in England produces 5,000,000*l.* yields little more than 500,000*l.* in India. The amount, therefore, which can be raised by any form of direct taxation in India is, in consequence of the general poverty of the country, extremely small; and the amount which can be raised by indirect taxation may be regarded as having already nearly reached its utmost possible limits. Nothing more than a very trifling amount can ever be raised by imposing taxes on luxuries which are consumed by the few. The indirect taxes which are really productive are those which are imposed on articles of general consumption. In India the mass of the people are so poor that they use no article which can be taxed except salt, and the taxation on salt has already reached that extreme point when any increase of duty would seriously diminish consumption. Lord Lawrence, in the evidence he gave before the Indian Finance Committee in 1873, had his attention specially directed to the question of obtaining additional revenue by increased taxation in India. It will be generally admitted that, from his long official experience, and from his intimate knowledge of the habits and feelings of the Indian people, no one could speak on such a subject with greater authority than Lord Lawrence, and he unhesitatingly said: "I am not prepared to mention any new sources of revenue which I think it would be politic to make use of. Succession duties, and the tobacco-tax, and so forth, have been constantly talked of; but we went into the subject very carefully, and came to the conclusion, almost unanimously, that it was unwise to introduce such taxes."[1] As since this evidence was given, the suggestion has from time to time been revived that a tobacco duty should be imposed in India, it is desirable to refer to the reasons that were urged against it by Lord Lawrence. He showed that, in order to levy it, it would be necessary either to increase the assessment on the land on which it was grown—and this would be interpreted as an augmentation of the land revenue—or to levy an excise duty on tobacco. As tobacco is freely grown in all the native states whose boundaries are conterminous with our own territories, it would become requisite, in order to prevent the importation of tobacco from these states, to establish customs lines extending over thousands of miles. As, moreover,

[1] See Report of Committee on East India Finance, 1873, p. 330.

tobacco is often grown by the Indian people for their own use, it would in all probability be found essential, in order to prevent the evasion of the duty, to make the growth of tobacco a Government monopoly. Scarcely any arrangement that could be adopted would be regarded as more harassing by the people of India. The opinion of other high authorities against a tobacco duty might be quoted. Thus Sir Donald McLeod, who was for many years Lieutenant-Governor of the Punjaub, and who was admitted to be one of the ablest financial administrators India ever produced, objected to the tax, and when examined before the Finance Committee directed its attention to an elaborate minute that had been prepared condemnatory of a tobacco duty, by Mr. (now Sir John) Strachey.

Unless it can be shown that the description which has been here given of the financial condition of India is inaccurate, I think it must be admitted that the subject is one which should cause the gravest anxiety. But it will probably be said: If the finances of India are in so critical a condition, can nothing be done? Can no effort be made to avert impending embarrassment? Of all the things connected with the financial administration of India that require to be done, nothing is so essential as the immediate recognition of the fact that India has hitherto been governed on far too costly a scale. Her position is like that of a landowner who has been living beyond his income. Each year some new mortgage has to be raised to make good the deficiency; and as the interest on these successive mortgages accumulates, and as there is no reduction but rather an increase in the scale of his expenditure, his estate steadily becomes more burdened with debt. To add to his difficulties, he has borrowed large sums of money to carry out various improvements; and, however desirable these improvements may be, many of them do not pay the interest on the capital expended. If, under such circumstances as these, a practical man of business were called in to advise what ought to be done, it is obvious that he would insist above all things that expenditure should be reduced. He would probably soon discover that, which is usually the case when a man lives beyond his means, that in all directions too much money had been spent. There would be no chance of placing the estate in a secure position, unless its owner were prepared by rigorous retrenchment to bring his expenditure well within his income. Mortgages might then be gradually reduced, and when a surplus had been secured many improvements might be carried out which could not prudently be undertaken when there was a risk that they would burden the property with a still heavier load of debt. The remedy which would have to be applied under the circumstances just described not inaccurately represents what is necessary to be done in order to place the finances of India in a sound position. For some years the Indian Government has been living beyond its means. In almost every direction too much money has been spent; and those who have been responsible for this expenditure seem too often to have forgotten that India, instead of being one of the wealthiest, is one of the poorest countries in the world. Page after page might be filled with instances of reckless extravagance. At one time a private irrigation company with a capital of a million, the 100*l.* shares of which are unsaleable at the nominal quotation of 60*l.*, is bought by the Indian Government at par, and in addition a large bonus is given to be distributed among the officials of the company. At another time 175,000*l.* is expended in building and furnishing a country house for the Governor of Bombay. It is no exaggeration to say that it would not be one half so mischievous to permit a million of English money to be spent in building a mansion for an English minister. It is quite within recent years that the Public Works Department has assumed its present large proportions. No care apparently has been taken to adjust the supply of highly paid European officers in this department to the demand, and it is now admitted that there is a complete block in the higher grades of the service. Employment cannot be found for many who are drawing large salaries from Indian revenues, and it is acknowledged that many are simply holding on to become eligible for pensions. But it is not simply that money has been thus recklessly squandered. It is just the same with a nation as it is with an individual. Whether or not a particular outlay can be justified depends upon the amount of income out of which it has to be made. Nothing, for instance, may be more appropriate than for a man with 4,000*l.* a year to live in a house the rent of which is 400*l.* But if his income is only 1,000*l.*, to live in such a house would be an act of reckless folly. It is no use to dilate upon the advantages which a man would derive from keeping a carriage. If he cannot afford a carriage, he must submit to the discomfort of a cab. Without an hour's delay the fact should be recognised that India is not in a position to pay for various services which she receives at their present rate of remuneration. A most important saving might be effected by more largely employing natives in positions which are now filled by highly paid Europeans, and from such a change political as well as financial advantages would result. A single example will show the great economy which might thus be effected. Mr. Rendel, Consulting Engineer of the East Indian

Railway Company and of the Government Railways, stated in his evidence before the Public Works Committee in 1878 that three years ago not a single native engine-driver was employed in India; that on one railway, the East Indian, 150 are now employed, and that the saving thus effected is 15,000*l.* a year. Mr. Rendel added that the European is paid at least ten times as much as the native driver, and "the native does a lot more work—he works longer hours and gives less trouble. We are entirely satisfied with the native drivers."

It is, however, scarcely necessary to remark, after what has been said about the present and prospective cost of the Indian army, that excessive military expenditure has done more than anything else to create the present financial embarrassment. It is particularly to be borne in mind that the great increase in this branch of expenditure has not been brought about by its being necessary for India to maintain a larger army. A few years after the abolition of the East India Company, what is known as the army amalgamation scheme was carried out in direct opposition to the advice of the most experienced Indian statesmen. India was thus, as it were, bound hand and foot to our own costly system of army administration, without any regard apparently being had to the fact that various schemes of military organisation, which may be perfectly suited to a country so wealthy as England, may be altogether unsuited to a country so poor as India. A single example will show to what an extent the pecuniary interests of India may, under the present system, be sacrificed. When, a few years since, the plan of short service was introduced, it was solely considered as an English question, and not a thought was apparently given to the effect it would have upon India. It need scarcely be said that a more costly scheme for India could hardly have been devised. The shorter the term of service the greater must be the charge for transport; and the men, after they have completed a short term of service, are a reserve ready at hand for England, but many thousands of miles away from India. I cannot do more on this occasion than thus incidentally allude to the question of army organisation, with the view of showing that, in order to reduce the military expenditure of India, it is not necessary to diminish the numerical strength of the Indian army. It is, however, not to be forgotten that most distinguished Indian statesmen have declared that it would be far better to incur whatever risks may be involved in the reduction of the Indian army, than to face the danger which is certain to arise from an increase of taxation in India. No man could be less likely than Lord Canning inconsiderately to recommend a reduction in the Indian army, for he

F 2

was Viceroy during the troublous days of the Mutiny; and yet Lord Canning unhesitatingly affirmed, and the opinion has subsequently been endorsed by Lord Northbrook, that if it were a question between imposing new and irritating taxes in India, such as the income-tax, "danger for danger, he (Lord Canning) would prefer to reduce the army." It is well known that an equally strong opinion as to the peril of adding to the taxation of India was expressed by Lord Mayo, a Viceroy who was alike distinguished for prudence, courage, and common sense. He had the sagacity to see that taxation in India could not be regarded as simply a financial question, but that it involved political consequences of the gravest moment. In a passage which has been often quoted, he said that it was almost impossible to exaggerate the discontent which was produced among all classes in India, both European and native, by the "constant increase of taxation which had for years been going on." Deaf to these warnings, instead of anything effectual having been done to arrest the growth of taxation, the financial position of India now is far more unsatisfactory than it was in Lord Mayo's time. Not only has there been an increase of Imperial taxation—new and irritating taxes, such as the licence tax, have been imposed—but in recent years the country has been enveloped in a network of local taxation. Lord Northbrook, in

August, 1878, in presenting an important petition from India in the House of Lords, endorsed the statement that "within the last seven years, in Bengal alone, there has been an increase of about a million, and for the whole of India more than three millions, per annum by provincial taxation."

When such opinions as these have been expressed by those who must be regarded as the very highest authorities on all questions affecting the government of India, it is not too much to say that the very existence of our rule in India may be gravely imperilled unless the finances of that country are placed in a more satisfactory position. The English people should awaken to the fact that the question is one which vitally concerns themselves as well as the people of India. There is scarcely any event which would bring greater discredit and greater misfortune on England than for the Indian Government to be forced to say: "Our financial exigencies are such that it is impossible to pay our way without coming to England for pecuniary aid." A burden might thus be cast upon English taxpayers which they would find hard to bear, and the consequences to India would be still more disastrous; for from the hour in which she was obliged to seek subventions from England, her virtual insolvency would be proclaimed. Before it is too late, England should resolve that such a contingency should be averted. Hitherto, it has unfortunately too frequently happened that the influence of England has been exerted not to save, but to spend, the money of the Indian people. The well-known saying of one who held a high official position is only too true, that "Indian finance has again and again been sacrificed to the exigencies of English estimates." No one can reasonably desire that the English Parliament should perpetually meddle in the details of Indian administration. It should, however, never be forgotten that when the East India Company was abolished, the English people became directly responsible for the government of India. It cannot, I think, be denied that this responsibility has been so imperfectly discharged, that in many respects the new system of government compares unfavourably with the old. Figures have already been quoted to show to what a remarkable extent the cost of administration has increased since the East India Company was abolished. There was at that time an independent control of expenditure which now seems to be almost entirely wanting. It was, no doubt, intended, when the government of India by the Act of 1858 was transferred from the Company to the Crown, that the Council of the Secretary of State should exercise the same control over Indian expenditure, as had formerly been exercised by the Directors of the Company and by the Court of Proprietors. But gradually the influence and control of the Council have been so completely whittled away that it is now openly declared by a Secretary of State that he can spend the revenues of India, beyond her frontiers, without obtaining the consent, or even bringing the subject under the notice, of his Council. Whether or not the power thus claimed is really conferred upon him by the Act of 1858, and by Acts which have subsequently been passed, raises questions which I cannot attempt to enter upon here. The whole subject, however, of the inadequacy of the control now exercised on the expenditure of the revenues of India, is one that urgently demands the most careful investigation. Nothing can be more unsatisfactory than the present state of things. When the Secretary of State desires to avoid responsibility, he can shelter himself behind his Council; when he desires to act, untrammelled by their control and unhampered by their advice, he can ignore them as completely as if they did not exist.[1]

In attempting to direct attention to the present financial condition of India, I am chiefly desirous

[1] The inadequacy of the control exercised over the financial administration of India by the Act of 1858, and the Acts subsequently passed, has been referred to in the Introduction to this volume.

to show how important are the issues involved, and how urgently the subject demands prompt consideration. Englishmen of all political parties are alike anxious that no misfortune should befall our Indian Empire. Opinions may differ as to the importance to be attributed to certain dangers with which she is sometimes said to be threatened; but no one can deny the reality of the peril which will be brought upon her by financial embarrassment; and the day, I believe, is not far distant when, with common consent, it will be said that those are the wisest governors of India who act steadily upon the maxim of a great statesman, that "finance is the key of England's position in India."

II.

THE INDIAN BUDGET OF 1879.[1]

In the previous Essay, I endeavoured to describe the financial condition of India, and I hope to be able in the following remarks to show the additional light which has been thrown on the present financial condition of that country by the budget which has been lately introduced at Calcutta, and by the financial arrangements which it is proposed to carry out both in England and India during the present year. The simple announcement that an exceptionally large addition to the indebtedness of India is to be accompanied not by an increase, but by a remission of taxation, is sufficient to show the extreme gravity of the financial situation in India. During the current year it is proposed to raise a $4\frac{1}{2}$ per cent. loan of 3,500,000*l.*[2] in India; the

[1] May, 1879.

[2] The amount of the loan to be raised in India is 5,000,000*l.*, and not, as here represented, 3,500,000*l.* It appears, however, from the budget statement for 1879-80, recently issued at Calcutta (see paragraph 268), that about 1,500,000*l.* of the 5,000,000*l.* which it is proposed to borrow is "needed to discharge, on the 1st of May next, the untransferred portion of the $5\frac{1}{2}$ per cent. loan," and,

Government have already announced their intention to introduce into the House of Commons a Bill which will authorise the Indian authorities to borrow 10,000,000*l.*[1] in England; and 2,000,000*l.* is to be advanced, free of interest, by England to India, as a contribution towards the expenses of the Afghan war. It therefore appears that in a single year it is proposed either to borrow, or to take authority to borrow, no less a sum than 15,500,000*l.*, an amount which represents more than one-tenth of the entire national debt of India. If it were possible to obtain additional revenue by fresh taxation, no one can suppose that the Indian Government would be so improvident as to sanction proposals which will cause such a large addition to be made to Indian indebtedness, without making any attempt to supply, by increased taxation, a portion of the deficit which has to be met. It may, therefore, be concluded that, in the opinion of the Indian Government, the extreme limit of taxation has now been reached in that

therefore, the "net amount thus called for is only 3,500,000*l.*" I am so anxious not to overstate the financial exigencies of India, that I accept this conclusion, although it is important to bear in mind, as appears from the same paragraph of the budget statement, that the necessity of raising a still larger loan to meet this year's heavy deficit has only been avoided by resorting to the temporary expedient of providing 1,200,000*l.* "from the public balances."

[1] This amount, after a strong remonstrance from the House of Commons, was eventually reduced to 5,000,000*l.*

country, and that, unless expenditure can be reduced, there is no margin from which to make any provision for such contingencies as war and famine, which we are officially told are certain to recur. Constant borrowing must consequently be regarded as the normal condition of Indian finance.

Although it may be thought that nothing can exceed the seriousness of the state of things thus disclosed, the outlook for the future becomes even much worse when it is seen that, in the midst of this embarrassment, the Indian Government are surrounded with influences that compel them to surrender a portion of the revenue, which they themselves admit is altogether inadequate to satisfy the demands now made upon it. The import duties on cotton goods are, during the present year, to be partly remitted, at a cost to the Indian revenue of about 150,000*l.*, which next year will be increased to 200,000*l.* No one for a moment will even pretend to say that, in the present state of Indian finance, the idea would have been entertained of remitting these duties if the finances of India were administered in the interest of that country alone.

The partial remission of these duties has been defended on the ground that they are protective in their character, and that it is wrong for free-trade England to sanction, in any form, the continuance of a protective duty. It is not, I believe, difficult to show that these duties are much less protective than is ordinarily supposed. It is important to bear in mind that in the Bombay mills, which are said to enjoy protection at the expense of Lancashire, the manufacture is almost entirely confined to the coarser sorts of cotton goods, upon which, when imported, no duty is imposed. But even if it is admitted that the import duties on cotton goods are as protective as they are alleged to be by the representatives of the manufacturing interest in England, it would be necessary, in order to justify the repeal of these duties, to show either that India could spare the revenue which they yield, or that it could be obtained in some other less objectionable form. When it is remembered that not a single year passes without a most serious addition being made to the indebtedness of India, it at once becomes evident that, as India has no surplus, she cannot surrender a single shilling of revenue without an equivalent amount being added to her debt. As long, therefore, as the state of Indian finance is such that she not only has no surplus, but has annually to borrow in order to make good a heavy deficit, it is impossible to justify any remission of taxation, unless the sacrifice of revenue which such a remission involves is to be compensated for from some other source. No one, so far as I am aware, has suggested new taxation, by which it would be practicable to obtain the revenue which is yielded by these cotton duties. In considering questions of taxation nothing can be more unwise than to conclude that that particular tax must be the best which is most in accord with the principles of economic science. The tastes, the habits, and the wishes of the people on whom the tax is to be imposed ought to be most carefully considered, and I believe it will not be denied that of all the taxes which are levied in India, there are none to which the people of that country feel so little objection as the import duties on cotton goods. It is, moreover, particularly worthy of remark, that the repeal of these duties must certainly tend to create greater inequality in the incidence of taxation in India. It will be generally admitted that, owing to the difficulty of imposing taxes which reach the wealthy classes, an unduly large part of the revenue of India is contributed by those who are extremely poor. As the cotton duties are now almost entirely imposed on the finer sorts of goods, which are chiefly consumed by the rich, it is obvious that the repeal of these duties would reduce the amount of taxation paid by the wealthy, and would consequently still further increase the inequality in the taxation borne by the poor.

It is sometimes urged that the real objections to these duties are not adequately understood by the people of India, and that they fail to appreciate the loss that is caused to them by their continuance. But precisely the same remark holds true with regard to every country in which a protectionist tariff is maintained. The people of Canada, for instance, appear to be altogether insensible to the injury which they are about to inflict upon themselves, by the more onerous protective duties with which they seem determined to fetter their commerce. But even if India could afford the sacrifice of revenue which is involved in the reduction of the cotton duties, it is of the first importance most carefully to inquire whether there are not other taxes in India which could with greater advantage be reduced. It is now universally acknowledged, that no circumstance connected with the financial condition of India is so serious as the increased burden which is imposed upon her through the loss by exchange. It need scarcely be remarked that, in order to bring about a more favourable state of exchange, it is necessary either to increase the remittances which other countries have to make to India, or to diminish the remittances which India has to make abroad. If her export trade should increase, there will be a larger amount to remit to India. There will consequently be a greater demand for bills on India, and the price of these bills will advance; in other words, the exchange will become more favourable. At the present time an export duty is levied on rice and some other articles of Indian produce. If these export duties were repealed, the export trade of India might receive an important stimulus, and an influence would thus be brought into operation to diminish the loss by exchange which she now has to bear. The policy which is now being pursued by the Indian Government will produce an exactly opposite result. The reduction of the cotton duties will increase the imports into India. The amount, therefore, which India will have to remit to other countries will be proportionately increased; the demand for bills on India will consequently be diminished; and thus, at the very time when the loss by exchange is causing a most severe strain upon the finances of India, the Indian Government adopts a policy which not only involves an indefensible sacrifice of revenue, but which directly tends to create a still more unfavourable exchange.

Greatly as the remission of the cotton duties is, for the reasons just adduced, to be deprecated, there are other objections of a much more weighty kind to be urged against this needless sacrifice of revenue. The most prominent feature in the Indian Budget of 1878 was the formation of what was described as a famine fund. The present Finance Minister, Sir John

Strachey, came to the conclusion, after a careful and exhaustive review of the state of Indian finance, that, the ordinary revenue of that country being barely sufficient to meet its ordinary expenditure, there was no margin left from which any provision could be made for such contingencies as war and famine. During the past twelve years there have been four famines in India; and since 1873 the famine in Bengal and the recent famine in Southern India have entailed an expenditure of 16,000,000*l.* As there was no margin of surplus revenue from which this large expenditure could be provided, the money had to be obtained by borrowing, and the debt of India has been proportionately increased. In order to prevent the recurrence of such a state of things, it would obviously be necessary, in years in which there were no famines, to secure a surplus that would enable a fund to be formed, from which the money required for the relief of famine could be provided. After calculating the amount of famine expenditure during the period above mentioned, Sir John Strachey came to the conclusion that, in order to establish a fund adequate for the purposes intended, it would be necessary to obtain an additional revenue of about 1,500,000*l.* a year. In order to provide this extra revenue, a licence tax of about 2 per cent. was imposed, and this tax was made to reach those who earned no more than four shillings a week. New cesses were levied in Bengal and other parts of India; and although the salt tax was reduced in the parts of the country which paid these new cesses, an additional revenue was raised from salt, and the people of Madras and Bombay, who were just recovering from the effects of a most terrible famine, found the salt duty increased by no less than 40 per cent. It was so generally admitted that, in the present condition of India, nothing but extreme necessity could justify this new taxation, that the Government lost no opportunity of declaring that the money which was to be obtained from this new and exceptionally burdensome taxation, was to meet a national emergency, and that it should be scrupulously devoted to the relief of famine. Nothing could be more specific than the following declaration of the Viceroy :—

"The sole justification of the increased taxation which has just been imposed upon the people of India for the purpose of insuring their Empire against the worst calamities of future famine, so far as such an insurance can now be practically provided, is the pledge we have given that a sum not less than a million and a half sterling, which exceeds the amount of the additional contributions obtained from the people for this purpose, shall be annually applied to it. . . . We have pledged ourselves not to spend one rupee of the special resources thus created upon works of a different character."

When the nature of the new taxation which was imposed upon the people of India is considered, a most ready assent must be given to the opinion thus expressed by the Viceroy, that the "sole justification" for the taxation was to be found in the purpose to which it was to be applied. The trades licence tax is an income tax in its most aggravated form, for it is an income tax from which every official and professional income is exempted. I doubt if the English people would consider the gravest emergency to justify the imposition of an income tax which would fall upon almost every artisan, and would leave untouched the entire official class, all the officers in the army, and all professional men. The salt duty had, before its recent increase, been one of the heaviest imposts ever levied on a first necessary of life. And yet the starving millions of Madras and Bombay, when they were scarcely able to raise their heads from the terrible affliction that had visited them, were told that the salt duty was to be increased by 40 per cent. Under these circumstances it can be readily understood how necessary it was deemed by the Viceroy to endeavour to allay discontent, by giving the most distinct promises language could convey, that not "one rupee" of the money which was thus collected from the poorest of the Indian people should be devoted to any other purpose than providing a fund which might relieve their future necessities. The new taxes have been collected, and not a shilling of the money which they yield has been devoted to the purposes to which they were pledged. A few months after the famine fund was called into nominal existence, the invasion of Afghanistan was undertaken, and the fund was absorbed in defraying the expenses of this military expedition. It will perhaps be said that the whole of the famine fund has not been devoted to this purpose, and that a portion of it is to be devoted to the partial remission of the cotton duties; for if these famine taxes had not been imposed, the Indian Government would not have thought that they could possibly spare the 200,000*l.* which the reduction of these duties will cost the revenue of India. But whatever conclusion may be adopted as to the precise manner in which the money which was intended to create a famine fund has been spent, there can be no question that not a fraction of the new taxation which was imposed for famine purposes has been devoted to this object. The pledge which was made to the Indian people has been alike broken, whether the money which they have been called upon to contribute has been expended for military purposes, or has been spent in enabling the Government in part to satisfy the demands which have been so persistently pressed upon them by the cotton-manufacturing interest in England.

It may not improbably happen that, in discussions on Indian finance, the famine fund will be referred to as if it still had an existence. Financial complexity has apparently for some people a strange fascination; and there are those who always seem to cling to the belief, that a considerable improvement can be effected in the finances both of a nation and of an individual by a dexterous arrangement of figures. Nothing can be more precise than the declarations which were made when the famine fund was established, that a part of the additional revenue yielded by the new taxation should be devoted to the reduction of debt: The reductions in the debt which would thus be effected in the years when there were no famines would, it was supposed, be equivalent to the addition that had to be made to the debt when famines had to be relieved; and consequently, over a series of years, the relief of famine would involve no increase in the indebtedness of India. It is obvious that the whole of this arrangement at once falls to the ground when, as is the case during the present year, although there is no famine, the necessities of the Indian Government are such that, instead of the debt of India being diminished, it is proposed to make to that debt an unprecedentedly large addition. It may be urged that India, in the present state of her finances, cannot possibly do without the additional revenue which is obtained from the taxes imposed for the creation of a famine fund. But if this be so, then it is far better at once to recognise the fact that these new taxes have not been applied to the creation of a famine fund, but that they are required for the general purposes of the Indian Government; and amongst these purposes it is particularly to be noted that the one which is considered of most pressing urgency is to reduce the import duties on cotton goods.

Although the amount of revenue which will be lost through the reduction of the cotton duties is comparatively small, yet it is almost impossible to overestimate the importance of the principles involved in this particular financial measure. It at once suggests the inquiry, To what extent ought the interests of England to control the finances of India? Not only, as has been already shown, have the most positive promises which the Viceroy made to the Indian people been disregarded, but I think it will scarcely be denied that a resolution which, at the instance of the Government, was unanimously passed by the House of Commons, has been entirely set aside. On the 10th of July, 1877, a motion was brought forward demanding the immediate repeal of the cotton duties.

The Government resisted it, on the ground that India could not at that time afford such a sacrifice of revenue; and the truth of this was so generally recognised that, without one dissentient voice, it was affirmed that the repeal of these duties should be postponed until the financial condition of India became more satisfactory. Is it possible to point to one single circumstance, which would justify the conclusion that the finances of India are in a more satisfactory state now than they were two years since, and that India can now afford a sacrifice of revenue which she could not afford then? It is repeatedly said that the loss by exchange has done far more than anything else to cause embarrassment to Indian finance. In 1877 the loss by exchange was estimated at about 1,676,482*l.*; during the present year it is calculated that India will lose by exchange 3,900,000*l.* In 1877 the amount added to the debt of India was 6,380,000*l.*; during the present year the Indian Government desires to borrow, or take authority to borrow, no less than 15,500,000*l.* It is, however, needless to multiply examples to show that if in 1877 India could not afford to sacrifice any existing source of revenue, she is in a far worse position to afford such a sacrifice at the present time. On all sides opinions are now expressed about the state of Indian finance, which only a short time since would have been described as the idle forebodings of sensational alarmists. The following is a description of the budget of the present year by one who certainly cannot be regarded as a prejudiced critic of the Indian Government :—

"The Indian press and the public continue to discuss the Financial Statement, and all classes, both European and native, show singular unanimity in condemning it, all sides describing it as the most melancholy, the most disheartening, and the most unstatesmanlike ever issued by the Government since the budget system was introduced."[1]

Although the opinion may be readily endorsed that nothing can be more unstatesmanlike than to surrender revenue at the very time when an exceptionally large deficit has to be met by increased borrowing, yet I think it would be unfair to single out Sir John Strachey for special censure, and to assume that he, being Finance Minister, is solely responsible for the financial arrangements which he has had to propose. It is probably impossible for any one who is outside the Government properly to appreciate the difficulties with which the Finance Minister has had to contend. One of his predecessors in office not many years since bitterly complained of the "extent to which Indian

[1] *Times* Calcutta correspondent, in the *Times* of the 24th of March, 1879.

finance was often sacrificed to the exigencies of English estimates;" and, if there were no occasion for official reserve, the present remission of the duties on cotton goods would not improbably be referred to as an example of the "extent to which Indian finance has to be sacrificed to the exigencies of English" politics. Not only, therefore, would it be unfair to concentrate all the blame either upon Sir John Strachey or the authorities at Calcutta, but I think it would be unjust to hold the present Indian Government, whether at Calcutta or in London, solely responsible for the existing embarrassment in Indian finance. Some of the causes which have brought about embarrassment have no doubt been solely the creation of the present Government. They alone are responsible for the addition to the strength of the army, and the consequent increase in military expenditure, which are said to be rendered necessary by the attempt to secure a more "scientific" frontier for our Indian empire. There are, however, many causes that have contributed to bring upon India her present financial difficulties, which came into operation long before the present Government took office. Thus it will be generally admitted that, in order to place the finances of India on a more satisfactory basis, it is above all things essential to reduce her present excessive military expenditure, which absorbs no less than

45 per cent. of her entire net revenue. Although this expenditure must be increased by the addition to the strength of the army to which reference has just been made, yet, in order to effect any important reduction in the cost of the Indian army, it will be necessary fundamentally to change the present military system, and to undo a great part of the work which was done when, under the auspices of Lord Palmerston's Government, and in spite of the remonstrances of every Indian statesman of experience, the army amalgamation scheme was carried out, and India was compulsorily made a partner in all the costly military arrangements of England. Next to military expenditure it will, I think, be acknowledged that there is no question which more urgently demands immediate attention than the large outlay on public works which has been continued for many years in India. It cannot, however, be said that the present Government is more responsible than its predecessors for the policy, which has proved financially so disastrous, of borrowing large sums of money each year for the construction of public works, which, though called at one time "reproductive," and at another time "remunerative," seldom, as is now shown by official returns, repay even a small part of the interest on the capital expended. Then again, the present unfavourable exchange is due to many causes, some of which at

least are altogether beyond the control of the Indian Government. As already explained, an unfavourable exchange is a necessary accompaniment of a depreciation in the value of silver; and the present great depreciation in the value of silver is partly due to the discovery of new silver mines in the United States, to a falling off in the demand for silver consequent on a demonetisation of silver by Germany, and to the restriction of the silver coinage in those countries which have joined what is known as the Latin Union. Although the present unfavourable state of the Indian exchange is no doubt in part to be attributed to the causes just mentioned, yet as the rate of exchange is intimately connected with the amount which India has to remit to England, each addition to the home charges must make the exchange more unfavourable; and these home charges have been permitted to increase, not under one, but under successive Indian Governments.

If for no other reason, I should think it particularly important fully to acknowledge that the present Government is not solely responsible for the existing condition of Indian finance, because I believe it is almost impossible to exaggerate the harm that may be done, if, in attempting to remedy the present state of things, the subject is approached in a spirit of political partisanship. It is scarcely necessary to remark that when the financial condition of a country is such as that of India at the present time, it is impossible for her finances to be placed in a more satisfactory position unless a policy of rigorous retrenchment is carried out with the most persistent determination. Any government that is prepared to do this is certain to have to bear a load of unpopularity. Expenditure cannot be curtailed, salaries cannot be reduced, and unnecessary offices abolished, without producing a great amount of discontent, and without bringing into active operation the keen opposition of those who consider that they have a vested interest in the continuance of the present system. Far, therefore, from desiring in the slightest degree to add to the difficulties which have now to be encountered by those who are responsible for the finances of India, no effort should be spared to give every possible assistance to any ministry that is willing at once to frankly recognise the fact that India has hitherto been far too expensively governed, and that consequently it is necessary at all hazards to reduce expenditure by adopting a policy of the strictest economy. The financial proposals embodied in the budget of the present year unfortunately afford scarcely any indication that the extreme gravity of the present financial situation is adequately appreciated either by the Government at Calcutta or by the Secretary of State. With the single exception of a reduction of 1,000,000*l.* in the outlay on public works, it appears that no serious attempt is to be made to effect retrenchment in any other branch of expenditure. Enormous as have been the military charges during the last few years, there is only too much reason to fear that these charges are more likely to increase than to diminish. The Afghan war is estimated to cost 2,600,000*l.*, and I believe those military and financial authorities, on whose judgment most reliance is to be placed, unanimously agree that this is far too low an estimate of cost. Moreover, it is to be remembered that when this estimate was made it was assumed that the war was virtually concluded, and that our occupation of territory would be confined within, comparatively speaking, very narrow limits. The Prime Minister, speaking in the House of Lords (13th of February, 1879), said: "Her Majesty's Government have the satisfaction of feeling that the object of their interference in Afghanistan has been completely accomplished. . . . We have secured the object for which the expedition was undertaken, and we have obtained that frontier which we hope and believe will render our Empire invulnerable." There seems little chance that this confident expectation will be realised. As long as active operations have to be undertaken, a heavy outlay must be incurred, and, far from the war having been concluded, scarcely a day elapses without the news of some movement in the field, and of skirmishes more or less important. The negotiations with Yakoob Khan do not apparently promise so speedy a termination of the war as was expected; for it is now (May, 1879) stated that the Viceroy and his advisers consider it to be not improbable that, in order to bring Yakoob Khan to terms, it will be necessary, at least temporarily, to occupy Cabul. If such an onward movement is undertaken, it is obvious that all estimates of the cost of the war which were based on the calculation that peace was near at hand, and that our occupation of territory would, as was said by the Prime Minister in his speech already quoted, be confined to retaining possession of the "three highways which connect Afghanistan with India," will have to be entirely modified. An advance on Cabul might lead to a prolongation of the war, and might involve an expenditure so large that, in order to defray it, a very considerable portion of the 15,500,000*l.*, which the Indian Government propose to take authority to borrow during the present year, would have to be expended. It is therefore most important to bear in mind that, whatever may be the reasons which are put forward to justify the exceptionally large borrowing powers the Indian Government seek to obtain, almost the entire proceeds of the loans which they desire to have authority to raise may have to be devoted to meet the expenses of continued military operations in Afghanistan. I desire, however, on the present occasion not to discuss the subject from this point of view, because I think it is very important carefully to consider the reasons which are adduced by the Government in support of their financial proposals.

The reduction of the cotton duties having been already referred to, it will only be necessary to direct attention to the three different ways in which the Indian Government propose to borrow money during the present year. As already stated, a 4½ per cent. loan of 3,500,000*l*. is to be raised in India. Parliament is asked to give authority to the Indian Government to borrow 10,000,000*l*. in England, and 2,000,000*l*. is to be advanced, free of interest, by England to India, as a contribution towards the expenses of the Afghan war. Before the announcement was made that it was the intention of the Government to take authority to borrow the exceptionally large amount of 10,000,000*l*. in England, it was supposed that the entire borrowing operations of the year would be confined to raising a loan of 3,500,000*l*. in India. For some years past successive Secretaries of State have agreed that it is most important, both on political and financial grounds, not to increase the obligations of India in England. In a despatch to the Government of India, in which Lord Salisbury reviewed the budget of 1874, he declared it to be indispensable that none but works which were likely to prove remunerative should be constructed from borrowed money, and he insisted, with the utmost emphasis, that the money required for their construction should be obtained by loans raised in India and not in England. No one questioned the soundness of this policy, for the fact was beginning to be recognised that from political considerations it was not prudent to be constantly adding to the obligations incurred by India abroad. Upon financial grounds it was agreed to be equally important not to increase the Indian debt in England, because each addition to this debt, by increasing the amount which India had to remit to England, tended to produce a more unfavourable rate of exchange. It is obvious that the principles which were thus to regulate the future financial administration of India have been completely set aside, when, in a single year, it is sought to obtain authority to borrow in England more than twice as much as it is proposed to borrow in India. So far as can be ascertained, the only reasons which are alleged in explanation of this departure from the policy which was so distinctly enunciated by Lord Salisbury, are that it may be found difficult to borrow in India the whole amount required; and, secondly, that it is necessary to raise a large loan in England, in order that the Government may have a reserve to fall back upon, and so be enabled to withhold their bills from the market when the exchange is unfavourable. It will at once be seen that it is impossible for the Government to put forward the first of these pleas, without virtually endorsing all the most unfavourable opinions that have been expressed with regard to the state of Indian finance. If it is difficult for the Government to borrow comparatively so small a sum as 3,500,000*l.* from the people of India themselves, it is evident either that they are too poor to lend, or that they are unwilling to entrust their savings to the State. Again, it must be borne in mind that those who lend one year have probably so much less to lend the next year, and consequently, if it is now found difficult to borrow 3,500,000*l.* in India, there will be still greater difficulty in borrowing a similar amount hereafter. Unless, therefore, something is immediately done to place the finances of India on a sounder basis, the deficits which will have to be annually met must necessarily, in an increasing proportion, be made good by loans raised in England.

At the present time there appears unfortunately little ground for hope that there will be any diminution in the amount of the Indian deficits. As already stated, it appears that no attempt is to be made to carry out in any of the spending departments such a policy of rigorous economy as India urgently needs; and, serious as is the loss which she now has to bear in consequence of an unfavourable exchange, I believe it can be shown that it is only too probable that the financial proposals which are now brought forward will, if they are carried out, exercise a very material influence in making the exchange even more unfavourable than it now is. If 10,000,000*l.* is borrowed in England, the financial position of India may no doubt for a time be made to wear a somewhat improved appearance. But the improvement will be just as unreal as if an embarrassed landowner, in order to meet his pressing obligations, raised another mortgage on his estate. It cannot be too persistently pressed on those who have to administer Indian finance, that each addition which is made to the debt of India in England must increase the amount which has to be transmitted, in the form of interest, from India to England. If, therefore, by devoting the proceeds of a loan to meet the obligations of India in England, the amount of bills on India which the Secretary of State has to sell in London is diminished, the relief can only be temporary; the loss by exchange is diminished this year only to be increased in future years. In defence of such a policy it is said, "something may happen." The Government at Calcutta seem to derive the greatest encouragement from the fact, that they have been informed that the Secretary of State and his council are taking the relative value of gold and silver into their consideration; and this is apparently regarded as such a hopeful omen for the future, that revenue is sacrificed at the very time when a great amount of additional indebtedness is being incurred. The relative value of gold and silver is determined by precisely the same laws as those which regulate the value of any other products. If, compared with gold, there is a large increase in the supply of silver, accompanied by a considerable falling off in the demand, a Secretary of State is just as powerless to arrest a depreciation in the value of silver as he is to stop the flow of the tide. It has sometimes been suggested that an Act of Parliament should be passed to fix the relative value of gold and silver, by declaring that so many rupees should be always worth a sovereign. Such a proposal is not less unreasonable than it would be to enact that, whatever the seasons might be, whether the harvest was good or bad, a sack of wheat should always exchange for a ton of coal. Such tampering with values can produce no other result than, by creating confusion and spreading a feeling of distrust, to aggravate the evils which it is sought to remedy. If silver becomes depreciated, there is only one way of restoring its value, and that is by acting either on the supply or the demand. In consequence of the large amount of silver, variously estimated at from 15,000,000*l.* to 20,000,000*l.*, that has been accumulated in Germany since silver was demonetised in that country, the supply of silver which can now be brought into the market depends to a considerable extent upon the German Government. The influence, however, which can thus be exerted upon the supply of silver must be regarded as temporary and accidental. The supply of silver is determined by precisely the same natural laws as those which regulate the supply of any other similar commodity. If new and more productive mines are discovered, the supply of silver will increase. If, however, the value of silver becomes depreciated, the profit obtained from existing mines will diminish, and the supply will consequently decrease.

It, therefore, appears that it would be alike unwise and futile to make any attempt to regulate the supply of silver. So far as the supply of silver depends upon the action of the German Government, we have, obviously, no power to exercise any control. Whatever may be our wishes on the subject, Germany will treat the disposal of her silver as a purely commercial transaction, and will bring her silver into the market at whatever time she thinks she will be able to sell it to the most advantage. It seems only too probable that the first effect of the policy which the Indian Government now seem anxious to carry out, may be to enable Germany to dispose of a large portion of her silver at a better price than she is now able to obtain. As already stated, if an Indian loan of 10,000,000*l*. is raised in England, the Government will be able for a time to withhold their council drafts from the market; the rate of exchange will improve, and the price of silver will advance. Germany will not be slow to take advantage of this advance; she will at once bring a large quantity of silver into the market; the price of silver will again fall; and the chief effect of the loan will have been to enable Germany to sell a portion of her silver on better terms, while India will be left to meet her increased obligations with the price of silver still further reduced, and the exchange made more unfavourable than before.

Although, therefore, from the considerations just adduced, it appears to be of the first importance not to attempt artificially to regulate the supply of silver, yet much can undoubtedly be done by Government action to affect the demand for silver, and consequently to influence its value; and I believe it can be shown that the Indian Government can exert a special influence on the demand for silver. Allusion has already been made to the heavy duty, amounting in some instances to 10 per cent., that is imposed on so important an article of Indian export as rice. If the state of Indian finance permitted this duty to be repealed, the export trade of India might be considerably developed, and the extra amount which would be required to pay for the additional quantity of produce exported would proportionately increase the demand for silver. But this is by no means the only way in which the demand for silver may be influenced by the action of the Indian Government. With regard to various proposals which are from time to time brought forward to deal with the Indian currency, it may be remarked that they one and all labour under the fatal defect, that instead of increasing, they would materially diminish the demand for silver, and thus ultimately lower its value. It has, for instance, been suggested that a gold currency should take the place of silver in India, and that the amount of the silver coinage should be restricted. But if these measures were carried out, it is evident that one of the largest of the existing sources of demand for silver would be to a great extent closed, and silver might become indefinitely more depreciated in value than it is even at the present time. As previously explained, the chief cause of the falling-off in the Indian demand for silver arises from the curtailment of her export trade, and from the constant increase in the amount which India has annually to remit for payments in England. The only legitimate method, therefore, which can be adopted to increase her demand for silver is to stimulate her export trade, and to diminish the amount of the home charges. Unfortunately, the course which is now being taken by the Indian Government, instead of diminishing, will seriously augment these home charges. If sanction is given to the proposal to raise a loan of 10,000,000*l.* in England, provision will have to be made to pay the interest on this loan; an additional sum of at least 400,000*l.* a year will consequently have to be transmitted from India to England, and the demand for silver will be lessened by this amount. Again, the 2,000,000*l.* which during the present year is to be advanced by England to India to assist her in defraying the expenses of the Afghan war will give her some temporary relief, but the relief can only be temporary; it will add to her difficulties in the future, because, as the money advanced is to be repaid in seven equal annual instalments, India will, during each of the next seven years, in addition to the other home charges, have to transmit about 300,000*l*. Such an arrangement only affords another example of the many that may be given to show that at the present time the difficulties of Indian finance, instead of being fairly faced, are merely being trifled with; but it cannot be too distinctly stated that, however heavily and recklessly the future may be discounted, a day of reckoning must inevitably come. Unless all considerations of prudence are to be completely set aside, it is evident that as the excessive amount of the home charges is embarrassing Indian finance by causing the serious loss by exchange, the greatest care should be taken, not only that another shilling should not be added to these charges, but that effectual measures should at once be adopted to diminish their amount.

It is often stated that the home charges do not admit of any important reduction, because, to a great extent, they represent payments for liabilities which have already been incurred. Thus, it is said, the interest must be paid on money which has been borrowed, and faith cannot be broken with those who are entitled to pensions. No one, of course, can be so unreasonable as to suggest that a policy of repudiation should be adopted, and that India should not meet the obligations which have been incurred on her behalf. Such considerations as these, however, do not in the slightest degree affect the importance of preventing in the future that which has happened in the past. Nothing can more conclusively show the peril involved in adding to the debt of India, than the fact that the interest which she has annually to pay on the debt already incurred imposes on her a burden which she finds it difficult to bear. The pensions and allowances which she has undertaken to grant must of course be paid; but if these pensions and allowances throw upon her a charge altogether disproportionate to her resources, an irresistible argument is at once supplied in favour of a fundamental change in the system. Taking the figures of the actual expenditure in 1876–77, the latest year for which they are available, it appears that no less an amount than 2,800,000*l.* of the revenues of India has annually to be paid in England in pensions, and furlough, compassionate, and absentee allowances. The real significance of this drain upon the resources of the country will be understood, when it is remembered that her entire net or available revenue is not more than 38,000,000*l.* The home charges for the army are constantly increasing. In December, 1877, the present Finance Minister, in bringing forward his financial measures for the creation of a famine fund, said: "I examined in some detail, in my minute laid before the Council on the 15th of March, the accounts of the army. I showed that it now costs upwards of 17,000,000*l.* a year; that its cost has increased by upwards of 1,000,000*l.* since 1875–76; and that a large share of this increase is in the expenditure recorded in the Home Accounts." Sir John Strachey added: "I do not assert that the whole of the additional expenditure on the army has not been incurred for excellent objects, or that it could have been avoided; but that the Indian revenues are liable to have great charges thrown upon them without the Government of India being consulted, and almost without any power of remonstrance, is a fact the gravity of which can hardly be exaggerated." Serious as is the state of things just disclosed, it is not difficult to understand how it has been brought about. Change after change is introduced into the organisation of our army, without a moment's thought being given to the effect which will be produced on Indian finance. A large part of the increase in the home military charges, to which reference has just been made, is no doubt to be attributed to the short-service system which has lately come into operation. As previously remarked, although short service may be an excellent arrangement for England, it was scarcely possible to have devised a more costly scheme of army organisation for India; and yet it appears from evidence given before a parliamentary committee by Sir Thomas Pears, late Secretary of the Military Department at the Indian Office, that there is no official record that the influence which would be exercised on the finances of India by the short-service system was ever considered by the English Government.[1]

Although it may be fairly contended that, whatever reforms in administration are introduced, a considerable time must elapse before such great items of charge as those just referred to can be materially reduced, yet an important saving might at once be effected if the work of retrenchment were vigorously taken in hand. An examination of the home charges will at once show that a year never elapses without various acts of extravagance being sanctioned. In some instances the amounts involved may be small, but it not unfrequently happens, that the want of due economy is most strikingly brought to light by some transaction in which the expenditure involved is not large. I might quote almost innumerable examples to show this. Looking over the latest accounts of the home

[1] See Report of East India Finance Committee, 1874, p. 53.

charges, it will be found that India is charged 1,200*l.* for the "Passage and Outfit of a Member of the Council of the Governor-General." In the same year she is charged 2,450*l.* for the "Passage and Outfit of the Bishops of Calcutta and Bombay and Chaplains."[1] But if any one requires to have brought home to him the lavishness with which the money of India is spent, it is only necessary to pay a visit to the India Office, and remember, as we pass along its spacious corridors, that that palatial building was erected by the Indian Government, and its costly establishment is maintained at the expense and for the use of one of the poorest countries in the world.

In thus directing attention to the great importance of reducing the home charges, it must not be

[1] An attempt has been made to justify these charges, on the plea that they are "fixed by Act of Parliament." (See speech of Mr. E. Stanhope, House of Commons, 22nd of May, 1879.) It is, however, obvious that if such a plea is brought forward, the Indian Government must accept one of these two alternatives—either they must consider the charges are not justifiable, and then it is their duty at once to propose the repeal of the Acts by which they are enforced; or if they consider the charges are justifiable they then make themselves just as responsible for the continuance of the charges as if the Acts by which they are imposed had never been passed. It appears from the Finance accounts that India, in 1877-8, had to pay 158,039*l.* for ecclesiastical charges. It is unnecessary to remark that none of this money is devoted to the support of the religions of the people of India.

supposed that this policy of retrenchment ought alone to be carried out with regard to the expenditure of Indian revenues in England. I have, however, in the previous essay, referred to the general costliness of Indian administration, and I have thought it important to make here special reference to the home charges, because the chief object which the Government seem anxious to obtain is a diminution of the loss by exchange, and there is, I believe, no hope that the exchange will become more favourable, unless the home charges are reduced. I trust it will not be thought that I underrate the difficulties which will have to be encountered, in carrying out a policy of rigid economy in the administration of Indian finance. Many who, until quite lately, always spoke of India as a country which could scarcely be administered on too liberal a scale, are now going to the opposite extreme, and express the most alarmist views as to her future financial position. In some of the leading English journals scarcely a week elapses without reference being made to the hopeless embarrassment of the finances of India, and her future insolvency is alluded to as if it could not be averted. Although I do not share these desponding views, yet it must be evident that, unless something is promptly done, the financial condition of India will indeed soon become one of hopeless embarrassment. It is not more certain that a stone, if it is not checked in its fall, will gather increased momentum, than it is that the system, which is now to receive its greatest development, of perpetually adding to the indebtedness of India, will, if it is not arrested, soon burden her with charges which she will be powerless to meet. The simple truth cannot be too persistently insisted upon, that India, throughout every department, has of late years been far too expensively governed. Although great economies may be effected, the smallest saving should not be neglected, and to those who are responsible for the management of Indian finance the fact should ever be present, that India is so poor that the waste of a shilling of her money may be of far more serious consequence than the waste of a pound of the money of England.

As I have now considered three of the four financial proposals of the Indian Government for the present year, namely, the reduction of the cotton duties, the raising of 3,500,000*l.* in India, and the borrowing of 10,000,000*l.* in England, it only remains to say a few words on the last of the four proposals—the advance of 2,000,000*l.* by England to India, free of interest, as a contribution towards the expenses of the Afghan war. This advance may be regarded from two entirely distinct points of view. In the first place, it may be considered as a gift or a charitable offering; and, secondly, it may be looked on as a discharge of an obligation legally and equitably imposed on England to bear some share of the cost of the Afghan war. If no such obligation really rests on England, then this advance of 2,000,000*l.*, without interest, is a gratuitous sacrifice on the part of England on behalf of India. It is scarcely necessary to remark that the consequences involved in the grant of such a subvention are most serious. The financial relations between England and India are at once placed on an entirely new footing. The Indian Government, by the acceptance of such an eleemosynary loan, virtually confess that the strain now put on the finances of India is more than she can bear, and that she is obliged to come to England for assistance. Not only is it an admission of financial exhaustion, but the granting of such assistance may produce a most disastrous effect upon the future financial administration of India. If the idea is once permitted to spread that the Indian authorities, whenever they are pressed for money, can draw upon the English Exchequer, every guarantee for economy will be swept away, and an incalculable injury may be inflicted both upon England and India.

It will, however, be probably said that the advance of this 2,000,000*l.* is not intended in any way as a gift, but that it must be solely regarded as a contribution, which England is legally bound to make, towards the expenses of the Afghan war. By the fifty-fifth section of the Government of India Act of 1858 it is distinctly provided, that when the Indian army is employed for imperial purposes beyond the frontiers of India the cost shall be borne by England, and when for Indian purposes the cost shall be borne by India. There seems to be no room for doubt that the present war has been undertaken, in part at least, for imperial purposes, and, therefore, India cannot be legally called upon to bear its entire cost. It has, in fact, been most distinctly stated by the Prime Minister that the military expedition into Afghanistan was not simply an Indian war, but was undertaken for imperial purposes; for, in a speech which he made in the House of Lords on the 10th of December, 1878, he said: "This is not a question of the Khyber Pass merely, and of some small cantonments at Dakka or at Jellalabad. It is a question which concerns the character and the influence of England in Europe." As no one would for a moment think of throwing upon India the entire cost of maintaining the influence and character of England in Europe, no other conclusion is possible, than that the advance of 2,000,000*l.*, without interest, to India is intended to be England's contribution towards the expense of an expedition which has been undertaken in the interest of the two countries. This being the case, it will be desirable to explain the exact share of the expense which will be borne by England and India respectively. As the 2,000,000*l.*, which England can borrow at 3 per cent., is to be repaid by seven equal annual instalments, and as the first instalment will become due at the end of next year, the amount which England will contribute by foregoing the interest on the loan is somewhat less than 320,000*l.* This sum, therefore, represents the amount which England will pay towards the expense of an expedition which, it is officially stated, will cost 2,600,000*l.*, and which, in the opinion of almost all independent military authorities, will greatly exceed this amount. But, assuming that the official estimate should prove strictly correct, it appears that India will pay 2,280,000*l.* and England 320,000*l.* India, therefore, will contribute more than seven pounds for every pound that is contributed by England. It is scarcely credible that a proposal should have been brought forward which would lead to such a result. It is, perhaps, only fair to conclude that when the real nature of the scheme is understood it will be promptly abandoned. At any rate it is difficult to suppose that it will ever be sanctioned by Parliament.[1] The English people, whatever may be their faults, have never been charged, even by their bitterest detractors, with meanness. But it is not easy to see how we can escape from such a charge, if, when an expedition has been undertaken, not simply in the interest of India, but to maintain the "influence and character of England in Europe," we compel the Indian people, whether they wish it or not, surrounded as they are with poverty and financial embarrassment, to pay more than seven times as much as is contributed by all the wealth of England.

[1] The Bill which authorised this advance of 2,000,000*l.* to India was discussed in the House of Commons on the 25th of July, 1879, and a resolution against its second reading was defeated by the narrow majority of twelve.

III.[1]

THE NEW DEPARTURE IN INDIAN FINANCE.

It has been specially provided by the Government of India Act, of 1858, that there shall be annually made in the House of Commons an Indian Financial Statement. Although the statement thus made is usually described as the Indian budget, the financial measures which constitute the budget arrangements for the year are first brought forward at Calcutta, and are generally in operation some time before the budget is considered in the House of Commons. The budget of 1879, which was discussed in the last Essay, was admitted on all sides to exhibit the financial condition of India in an extremely grave aspect. Hitherto the true character of the financial situation in India had been ignored by successive Governments; but when the time arrived for the discussion of the budget of 1879 in Parliament, the Government felt that they were brought face to face with a state of things so serious that they wisely resolved to abandon all attempts at palliation or excuse, and determined fully and frankly to

[1] October, 1879.

recognise the true character of the difficulties which had to be encountered. The admissions which were made on behalf of the Government were so unreserved that the discussion of the Indian budget of 1879 in Parliament will not improbably be long referred to as marking the commencement of a new epoch in Indian finance.[1] As previously remarked, the true financial condition of India had never up till this time been officially recognised. Liberal and Conservative Governments had not only persistently denied that there was anything in the state of Indian finance to cause apprehension, but year after year, as the time for the introduction of the Indian budget recurred, her actual financial condition was depicted in roseate hues, and her future was described in a spirit of increasing hopefulness. So little cause was there said to be for uneasiness or alarm, that the Indian budget used always to be postponed till a period of the session when all other important business had been disposed of. When the budget was considered, it was little more than a repetition of an oft-told tale. By classing some branch of

[1] The debate on the Indian budget of 1879 commenced at an unusually early period of the session (May 22nd), and the discussion excited such general interest that it was continued for three nights. This affords a striking contrast to what has taken place in previous years, when the Indian budget has generally been hurriedly considered in the closing hours of the session.

expenditure as "extraordinary," and by regarding some outlay as exceptional, the Indian accounts were almost invariably arranged so as to exhibit a surplus. The public works expenditure was habitually compared to the profitable investment of capital by a wise and beneficent landowner in the improvement of a judiciously-administered estate. A most significant change, however, has lately occurred. A large portion of the outlay on public works is now officially admitted to be unremunerative; and the Finance Minister, Sir John Strachey, has been forced to admit that a review of the finances of India for seven years, a period long enough to show their normal position, "made it plain that we possessed no true surplus of revenue over expenditure to cover the many contingencies to which a great country is exposed." Events which have recently happened only too clearly show that contingencies which may put a severe strain upon the finances of India may at any moment occur. When, a few months since, the war with Afghanistan was concluded, and the Treaty of Gundamuk was signed, there seemed some reason to hope that India might enjoy a period of peace and repose. It now, however, appears that the fanatical fury of a dissolute monarch may lead to another Burmese war; and the revolt at Cabul, by necessitating the renewal of hostilities in Afghanistan, involves an increase of expenditure, and may, if the greatest care and prudence are not shown, make a most serious permanent addition to the military expenditure of India.

In order still further to show the striking change of tone recently adopted by those who are responsible for the government of India, it is particularly worthy of remark that the Viceroy and the Secretary of State now unreservedly accept the conclusion that the limit of taxation has been reached in India, and that it has consequently become imperatively necessary that expenditure should be reduced. In a despatch which has been lately issued by the Viceroy and his Council to the local Governments, it is declared that "immediate measures must be taken for the reduction of the public expenditure in all its branches." On behalf of the Secretary of State it has been with equal positiveness announced that the balance between revenue and expenditure must be restored, not by the imposition of new taxation, but by "a large reduction of expenditure."[1] It is impossible to overestimate the importance of so full and frank a recognition of the real financial position of India. It is not too much to say that one obstacle which stood in the way of all attempts to reform Indian finance

[1] See Speech of Mr. Stanhope in introducing the Indian budget, May 22, 1879.

has now been surmounted. All experience, however, shows that any Government that is determined to carry out a policy of rigorous retrenchment will find itself beset by the most formidable difficulties. Devoted friends of economy in the abstract not unfrequently become its bitter assailants when the particular economy proposed happens to touch some branch of expenditure in which they themselves, either from pecuniary or philanthropic motives, are interested. Whatever may be thought of the previous mismanagement of Indian finance, nothing can be more useless than to indulge in vain regrets and recriminations about the past. Accepting unreservedly the promises which have been given that in the future a different policy shall be pursued, no effort should be spared to strengthen the hands of the Indian Government by rendering them every possible assistance in effecting those reductions in expenditure which they are now so absolutely pledged to secure.

From the reference that has just been made to the opinions recently expressed by the Governor-General and the Secretary of State, it not only appears that the necessity of immediately obtaining a large reduction of expenditure is fully acknowledged, but it can be shown that this reduction is a matter of such urgent importance that no excuse can be put forward to justify even its temporary postponement. In the memorandum of the Governor-General from which I have already quoted, it is stated that "rigid economy in every branch of the public service is, in present circumstances, the policy which must be followed. . . . . No fresh establishments must be entertained; no new offices must be created; no new works which it is possible to postpone must be commenced." And now it may be naturally asked, what are the circumstances which have induced the Government to adopt so entirely new an attitude with regard to Indian finance? As previously remarked, until quite lately, instead of a large reduction of expenditure being peremptorily insisted upon, expenditure was year after year permitted to increase without apparently exciting even a semblance of uneasiness. For some time past it has been the settled policy of the Government to borrow from four to five millions a year for the construction of public works. The importance of curtailing this outlay is now so fully acknowledged, that sanction has been given to the most drastic measures of retrenchment. The amount to be borrowed for public works is in no single year to exceed 2,500,000*l.*, and this limit is not to be exceeded even if its maintenance should involve the necessity of suspending works which are already in process of construction. It need scarcely be remarked that it would have been far better if this awakening to the real position of Indian finance had not been so long delayed. The difficulties of carrying out a policy of economy are indefinitely increased, if such a policy has suddenly to be introduced where before there have been carelessness and extravagance. However desirous the Indian Government may now be to reduce expenditure, they will find themselves perpetually hampered, and their efforts to save money constantly thwarted by the effects of past lavishness still continuing in operation. If costly establishments have been allowed to grow up, a large part of the expense which their maintenance involves will have to be borne long after it has been decided that these establishments shall be reduced. When a government finds that there are more persons in its employment than there is work for them to do, it cannot suddenly dismiss them without any compensation; pensions on a liberal scale have to be granted; and these pensions will for some time absorb a considerable part of the saving which may be ultimately secured. As an illustration of what has just been stated, it may be mentioned that the Government hope during the present year to obtain in the civil departments a reduction of expenditure which will amount to 1,000,000*l*. a year. A considerable part of this reduction, however, must be regarded as prospective, for the Governor-General admits that "there must be a serious set-off on account of pensions and other forms of compensation to the officers with whose services it will be necessary to dispense." Without desiring to make any unnecessary reference to errors that have been committed in the past, I think it is important to lay special stress upon the fact that the results of a policy of laxity and extravagance will cause a severe drain upon the resources of a country, long after such a policy has been replaced by one of the most rigorous economy. The special circumstances which are now imposing so severe a strain upon the finances of India may to a great extent cease to exist. If this should be the case, the necessity for care and thrift appearing not to be so pressing as it now is, the Government may drift back into its old course, and the present zeal for economy may pass away. The fact, however, should never for a moment be lost sight of, that new contingencies may arise; these may suddenly create financial difficulties as serious as those which now have to be encountered, and these difficulties will be indefinitely increased, if, in addition to the actual needs of the day, there has to be met in a season of adversity a considerable portion of the expenditure sanctioned in more prosperous times.

In endeavouring to give an explanation of the

causes which have produced the present remarkable change in the official view of Indian finance, it will not be necessary to attempt to apportion the exact amount of blame which may be fairly laid to the charge of successive governments, for having so long and so persistently given an inaccurate account of the financial condition of India. No useful end can be served by embarking on such a controversy. It may, no doubt, be fairly argued that some of the circumstances which, at the present time, are so prejudicially affecting the finances of India, have only recently come into operation; it would not, however, on the other hand, be difficult to show that for years past India has had no financial reserve, and that additional expenditure has consequently had to be met either by increased borrowing, or by imposing fresh taxation most burdensome to the people. But however greatly we may regret that those who have been responsible for the government of India should, during so lengthened a period, have administered her finances in a manner which has brought her to the brink of the gravest financial embarrassment, yet it may now be regarded as a subject for the most sincere congratulation that the peril of the situation has at last been recognised, and that efforts are to be made which, if steadily persisted in, will place her finances on a sound and satisfactory basis.

In enumerating the causes that have produced the striking change of opinion with regard to Indian finance to which reference has been made, chief prominence must be given to the four following circumstances, which I will proceed separately to consider:—

1. The necessity of providing for famines out of ordinary revenue, and the character of the new taxation which had to be imposed for the establishment of a famine fund.

2. The increasing loss by exchange.

3. The necessity of providing for the cost of the Afghan war by borrowing.

4. The unremunerative character of a large portion of the expenditure on public works.

With regard to the first of these causes, it may be mentioned that at the close of 1877 the Finance Minister, in view of the fact that in twelve years four famines had occurred in different parts of India, most wisely came to the conclusion that famines could not be treated as events of an exceptional character; but that, as they were certain to recur, the money which had to be spent in famine relief ought to be provided out of the ordinary revenue of the year. As the amount which had been expended in the two most recent famines, namely, those in Bengal and in Southern India, had been more than 15,000,000*l.*, he calculated that it would be necessary to provide out of ordinary revenue 1,500,000*l.* a year for the purposes of famine relief. It is supposed that if this sum is devoted to the reduction of debt in years when there are no famines, the debt might be reduced by an amount equivalent to the addition which has to be made to it in famine years, and thus the relief of famine over a series of years would involve no augumentation of the debt of India. But at the time when it was determined to devote this 1,500,000*l.* a year to the creation of a famine fund, the ordinary revenue was barely sufficient to meet the ordinary expenditure. As there was no surplus out of which the money could be provided, and as no material reduction in expenditure was attempted, it became absolutely necessary to obtain the larger portion of the money that was required by additional taxation. Of the 1,500,000*l.*, the sum which had to be provided by new taxation was 1,100,000*l.* It must, in justice to the Government of India, be assumed that before deciding as to the particular way in which this 1,100,000*l.* should be obtained, the entire fiscal system of India was most carefully reviewed, with the object of ascertaining what new tax could be imposed, or what existing tax could be increased with the least hardship to the people. It was ultimately decided that about two-thirds of the amount required should be procured by the imposition of a licence tax. Starting with the assumption that the Government came to the deliberate conclusion that the licence tax was the best and most available means of obtaining comparatively so small an addition to the revenue as 750,000*l.*, it will only be necessary to describe the nature and the incidence of this tax, and to refer to the deep discontent which the levying of such a tax is already producing among the people, in order to show with striking distinctness how nearly the limits of practicable taxation in India have been approached, and what incalculable evils may be produced, if, either from laxity or from any other cause, it should become necessary again to impose additional taxation in India. The licence tax as now levied is virtually an income tax of about fivepence in the pound imposed upon all those who derive an income from trade or from skilled labour. Professional and official incomes are entirely exempted from the tax. The Governor-General with 25,000*l.* a year, the officers in the army, the well-paid civilians, successful barristers and doctors do not contribute a farthing to the tax, but it is levied from every petty trader and every handicraftsman, although their scanty earnings may amount to no more than 4*s.* a week.[1]

[1] By a bill which was brought forward at a meeting of the Legislative Council of the Viceroy (Nov. 14, 1879) several weeks after this

But the inequality of such taxation and the severity of the burden which it imposes on those who are so poor that their income is only 10*l.* a year, may be regarded as by no means the most serious objection to such taxation. Although the tax has been in operation for little more than a twelvemonth, no one can deny that it has already produced a feeling of widespread and deep discontent, and facts can be mentioned which show that this discontent is far more due to the abuses inseparably connected with the levying of the tax than to the mere amount of the burden which the tax, if it could be fairly raised, would impose on the people. During many months the Indian papers have contained numerous instances of the tax being assessed at an excessive amount, and of its being levied on classes who were never intended to pay it. These newspaper reports are abundantly confirmed by communications which I have received from persons who hold high official positions in the Civil Service of India. I thus find it stated, on authority which cannot be disputed, that in one district in Bombay, out of 25,000 assessments made by one official nearly one half were appealed against, and in all these appeals the assessments had to be modified by the revising officer. It is well

essay was written, it is proposed to amend the Trades Licence Tax in many important particulars. These amendments are considered in the Appendix.

known that the cost and annoyance involved in these appeals are so great, that in a vast number of cases people submit to an unjust assessment rather than travel many miles and then incur the outlay and the worry of appearing in court to protest. The indefensible exemption of the official and professional classes from contributing to the licence tax converts it into an income tax in its most obnoxious form; and not only is this the case, but the present licence tax is levied with far more rigour than was the income tax when imposed in India a few years since. Although that tax was of the same nominal amount, it appears that the licence tax, in spite of its exemptions, enforces a much larger contribution from the mass of the people. Thus in the district of Mymensing the licence tax has been assessed at 158,373 rupees, whereas the income tax only produced 39,295 rupees. In Tangail 52,412 rupees are to be obtained from the licence tax, while only 10,752 rupees were produced by the income tax. When it is borne in mind that the official and professional classes, who are exempted from the licence tax, were assessed to the income tax, and that the net yield of the former tax is estimated to be considerably greater than that of the latter, it seems to be conclusively proved that the licence tax falls with extreme severity upon numerous classes of the very poor who were not reached by the income tax. It must moreover be remembered that throughout a considerable part of India the burden of this new taxation falls upon many who are only just recovering from the effects of a terrible famine.

The object I have in view in making these remarks is not to condemn the Government for imposing the licence tax. The more unreservedly we accept all that has been urged to justify what has been done, the more irresistibly are we led to the conclusion that the financial condition of India is one of such extreme peril that economy is not only desirable, but is a matter of imperative necessity. If, in order to increase the revenue by an amount comparatively so small as 750,000*l.*, the best course that can be adopted by the Government is to impose such taxation as that which has just been described, the question may be asked, to what straits may not the Government be reduced, if any fresh contingency, such as the renewal of hostilities with Afghanistan, should make it necessary to increase the revenue by an amount compared with which 750,000*l.* would be but a trifle? In order adequately to appreciate the financial situation in India, the answer which must be given to this question should never be absent from the thoughts of those who are responsible for the administration of her finances. If such an additional amount of revenue had to be obtained, we are brought face to face with these alternatives: either recourse must be had to some new form of taxation which is more objectionable than the licence tax, because, if it were not so, it would have been selected in preference to the licence tax; or the yield from the licence tax must be augmented either by increasing its rate, or by assessing it on incomes even smaller than those on which it is now imposed. Such considerations as these cannot have been absent from the minds of those who are responsible for the government of India, and, if they stood alone, they might be regarded as sufficient to account for the remarkable change in the official view which is now taken of Indian finance.

It cannot, however, be doubted that in considering the causes which have brought home to the Government the necessity of increased economy, a prominent position ought to be given to the serious loss which has resulted from a depreciation in the value of silver producing an unfavourable exchange. As I have already referred to this subject, it is not necessary again to explain in detail the manner in which a fall in the value of silver prejudicially affects the finances of India. As, however, the home charges have hitherto steadily increased, it may be desirable not only to show the manner in which the loss by exchange depends on the amount of these charges, but also to point out the direct influence which is exerted by any increase in these charges in depreciating the value of silver, and in thus adding to the loss by exchange. It is obvious that any country which receives its revenue in one metal and undertakes to make large payments in another, enters into a very speculative undertaking. If the value of the metal in which the revenue is received becomes depreciated when compared with the value of the metal in which payments have to be made, the real amount of these payments is proportionately increased. On the other hand, their amount will be diminished if the value of the metal in which the revenue is received becomes appreciated when compared with that in which payments have to be made. It is manifestly very undesirable that the fiscal system of a country should be deranged by such risks of loss and gain as those to which reference has just been made, and therefore the greatest care ought to be taken to prevent a country pledging itself to make unduly large payments in a metal different from that in which her revenue is received. It is now admitted that the entire net revenue of India is only about 38,000,000*l.* The whole of this revenue is received in silver, and more than one half of the amount has, in order to defray the home charges, to be devoted to make payments in gold. The net amount of these home charges during the present year has been officially stated at 17,000,000*l.* In calculating the Indian revenue in pounds sterling it is assumed that ten rupees are equivalent to one pound. The net revenue of India may therefore be stated as 380,000,000 rupees. But now that silver has fallen from what was long its normal value, about 60*d.* an ounce, to about 52*d.* an ounce, twelve rupees and not ten are equivalent to a pound sterling. In order therefore to make a payment of 17,000,000*l.*, 204,000,000 rupees are required, and it consequently appears that as the home charges now amount to 17,000,000*l.*, these charges absorb more than one-half the entire net revenue. As, therefore, India is liable to the most serious risks as long as so large a portion of her revenue has to be expended in making payments in gold, it is of the first importance that these home charges should not be permitted to increase, but measures ought at once to be taken to effect in them every possible reduction. During the last few years the home charges have increased to a most serious extent. It was shown by Mr. J. K. Cross, in the able speech which he made in the debate last session on the Indian budget, that the home charges, which in 1868 absorbed 43½ per cent. of the net land revenue, will during the present year absorb the whole of that revenue. The necessity of securing a reduction in the home charges is the greater, because each increase in them exerts a direct influence in still further depreciating the value of silver, and thus adds to the loss by exchange which India has to bear; while every reduction in the amount of these charges must exercise a corresponding effect in restoring the value of silver.

Any question referring to the value of the precious metals is liable to be so confused by the irrelevant intrusion of currency theories, that it cannot be too carefully borne in mind that the value either of gold or silver is regulated by just the same causes as those which regulate the value of any other commodity. If there is a diminution in the demand, or an increase in the supply, an influence is at once brought into operation to lower values. It has already been shown that many agencies have come into operation during the last few years which have caused an increase in the supply of silver to be accompanied by a considerable falling off in the demand, and thus a double influence has been exerted to lower its value. Amongst the many circumstances which have contributed to lessen the demand for silver, a position of chief prominence must undoubtedly be given to the great augmentation in the home charges during the past few years. It is well known that these charges are usually not defrayed by the remission of specie from India, but that bills drawn on India are sold by the Secretary of State in London. About 300,000*l*. worth of these bills are each week offered for sale. They are purchased by merchants and others who have payments to make in India, and as these bills thus take the place of specie, it is obvious that each increase in the amount of these bills proportionately diminishes the demand for silver to be transmitted to India. For many years the large loans which were annually raised in England for the construction of Indian railways to a great extent neutralised the prejudicial effect which is now exercised on Indian finance by the home charges. Previous to 1874, during a period of twenty years, a sum of not less than 5,000,000*l*. was on the average annually raised in England for the construction of guaranteed railways in India. Instead of transmitting this capital to India in the form of money, a very considerable portion of it was used to meet the home charges, and thus the amount of bills which had to be sold by the Secretary of State to defray these charges was proportionately diminished. This system of constructing Indian railways on the guaranteed system has been finally abandoned. It has also now been decided that when money is borrowed for public works in India, the loan should be raised there and not in England; and consequently, as the home charges will have in future to be entirely met either by the transmission of specie from India to England, or by the sale in England of bills drawn upon India, the prejudicial effect which must be exercised upon the rate of exchange will, unless these charges are diminished, continue with unabated force. For a long time the Government in India seemed to cling to the idea that by some artificial currency arrangement the value of silver could be restored, and the exchange rendered less unfavourable. It is unnecessary again to discuss the many theories which have from time to time been propounded. I believe it can be shown that any tampering with the currency would have indefinitely aggravated the evil it was sought to remove. No surer means can be adopted of still further depreciating the value of silver than to diminish the demand for it, and if any of the many proposals which have lately been propounded with regard to the silver question are considered, such, for instance, as the introduction into India of a gold currency, or the limitation of the amount of silver annually coined, it will be at once seen that all these suggested remedies alike labour under the defect that they could not be carried out without lessening the demand for silver. No circumstance that has recently occurred in connection with Indian finance is a subject for more sincere congratulation, than that it seems to have been finally determined by the authorities in England not to sanction any change whatever in the Indian currency. Independently of the objections to which allusion has just been made, it would be difficult to overestimate the mischief which would result from altering the currency of a people who are so stationary in their habits that they dislike change with an intensity which Europeans find it almost impossible to understand. A large majority of the population of India are cultivators of the land. They have entered into engagements to pay, either permanently or for a fixed period, a certain number of rupees to the Government for the land which they cultivate. If, because silver has become depreciated, they were ordered to make this payment in gold, or if they found that the weight of silver in the rupee was increased in order to get from them more silver than they had stipulated to pay, a feeling would spread among the people from one end of India to the other that they were the victims of a breach of faith; there would naturally arise the deepest distrust of the Government; and the harm that would be done would be indefinitely more serious than any mischief which can possibly result from the loss by exchange. It appears that India has had a very narrow escape from the danger to which reference has just been made. Up to the very last the authorities at Calcutta apparently indulged the hope that the loss by exchange might be averted by some currency device. Sir John Strachey, in his budget speech of the present year, refers with satisfaction to the fact that measures which were suggested by the Viceroy and his Council for dealing with the exchange difficulty were at the time under the consideration of the Secretary of State. It is well known that the suggestion to effect some alteration in the Indian currency was favourably entertained by some members of the Council of the Secretary of State, and by other authorities at the India Office. Fortunately, however, advice was sought from the outside; a departmental committee was appointed which comprised amongst its members some officials who were not connected with the India Office; and it is probable that to the investigations of this committee it is to a great degree due that the wise decision has been arrived at, that, so far as the currency is concerned, things must be left alone. The decision which was thus come to, seems at once to have produced a most marked effect. The authorities in India and in England had brought home to them with convincing force, that as the loss by exchange was a serious burden on the finances of India, which could not be lightened by any modifications of the currency, there would continue to be increasing deficits, unless measures were at once taken to reduce expenditure. Other difficulties, moreover, besides the loss by exchange had to be met. Provision had still to be made for the larger part of the expenses incurred in the Afghan war, and for years there had been carried on an expenditure on public works, which it was every day becoming more evident India could not afford.

With regard to making provision for the expenses of the Afghan war the difficulty has been rather evaded than encountered. Assuming that the cost of the war did not exceed the official estimate of 2,600,000*l.*, only one quarter of this amount has so far been provided by India, for 2,000,000*l.* has been lent to her free of interest by England. As this 2,000,000*l.* is to be repaid by India in seven years, the exact amount of the contribution which England will make to this war is less than 320,000*l.*, this sum representing somewhat more than the loss of interest on a loan of 2,000,000*l.* made in the manner just described. I do not here intend again to consider whether England in contributing 320,000*l.*, or less than a seventh of an aggregate expenditure of 2,600,000*l.*, is either legally or equitably bearing her proper share of the cost of a war which was said, both by the Viceroy and the Prime Minister, to have been undertaken for Imperial purposes. The question, however, as to the exact proportion in which the cost of pursuing a "forward policy" in Afghanistan should be borne by England and India respectively, will have again to be considered, now that it has become necessary to renew hostilities in Afghanistan.

The 2,000,000*l*, which has been thus advanced by England will no doubt afford India some temporary relief; but it is obvious that this relief is obtained by having recourse to the expedient of discounting the future. The loan will, during the present year, diminish by 2,000,000*l*. the sum which will have to be provided from India to defray the home charges, and in this way the rate of exchange may, to a certain extent, be favourably affected. During the next seven years, however, as the instalments for the repayment of the loan become due, India will have to provide the money for these payments, and consequently a more favourable exchange during one year is secured by making the exchange more unfavourable during the succeeding seven years. It is obvious that nothing but extreme necessity can be pleaded as an excuse for the adoption by any government of such financial expedients.

The fact that India has had to be assisted by England with a loan of 2,000,000*l.* affords a striking proof that, in considering all Indian questions, a position of first importance must be given to their financial aspects. In deciding upon any particular course of policy, the element of cost should never for a moment be absent. It may be premature to attempt to determine what should be our future action in Afghanistan under the present change of circumstances, but it cannot be too strongly insisted upon that, in the existing financial condition of India, no peril can be more serious than the adoption of a policy which, if it should lead to a large additional expenditure, would sooner or later necessitate an increase of taxation. It has already been shown that, to obtain the comparatively small sum of 750,000*l.*, the Government thought that the best course which was open to them was to impose the licence tax. In order to form an idea of what increased taxation may signify in India, it is only necessary to bear in mind the effect which this tax is producing, and to remember that, if fresh taxation has again to be resorted to, some impost even more obnoxious than the licence tax will have to be levied. Those who are most competent to form an opinion seem unanimously to agree that any policy which would lead to annexation in Afghanistan would cause a large permanent addition to the annual expenditure of India. If such a policy should be adopted, both the present Secretary of State and the Viceroy would stand self-condemned; for after the admissions which within the last few months they have so unreservedly made as to the financial condition of India, it is impossible for them to sanction new and heavy charges being thrown upon her, without the conclusion being ever present to their minds that the additional taxation which must be the inevitable accompaniment of increased expenditure will bring upon India the gravest perils.

It has been previously mentioned that in addition to the various unfavourable circumstances already enumerated, which brought home with striking distinctness to the Indian Government the present critical state of Indian finance, facts have gradually come to light which have led irresistibly to the conclusion that a large part of the outlay on works which are classed as "reproductive" does not yield even a small fraction of the interest which has to be paid on the capital borrowed for their construction. Early in the Session of 1878, the Under-Secretary of State for India, in moving for the appointment of a Select Committee to inquire into this public works expenditure, stated that on the 9,000,000*l*. spent in recent years on schemes of irrigation in Bengal, the return which is yielded is only $\frac{1}{2}$ per cent. This conclusion was abundantly verified after a most careful and exhaustive investigation of the entire subject by the committee which sat during the Sessions of 1878 and 1879. In their report, which has lately been published, and which was drawn up with much ability by the chairman of the committee, Lord George Hamilton, it is shown that, in the case of many irrigation works, the return which is yielded, far from paying the interest on the capital expended, does not even suffice to meet the working expenses. Some works of irrigation have undoubtedly proved to be very remunerative; but it is clearly shown by elaborate statistical returns which have been summarised in the report of the committee, that, with the single exception of the works in Scinde, the schemes from which large profits are secured are either old native works, like the Eastern and Western Jumna Canals, and the Cauvery anicut, which have been restored by British agency, or works which have been constructed under exceptionally favourable conditions, such as the Godavery and Kristnah. Thus, taking the year 1875–76, the latest for which the official figures are given, it appears that up to that time, without including the value of the old native works, 15,562,655*l.* had been expended on schemes of irrigation in India. The net return in that year on this outlay, after allowing for working expenses, was 832,243*l.* As 700,319*l.* would represent the charge for interest at 4½ per cent. on a capital of 15,562,655*l.*, it follows that the irrigation expenditure yields a net profit of 131,924*l.* But on further examination it is at once seen that, as previously stated, the whole of this profit is obtained from old restored native works, and from those which have been constructed in Scinde and in the deltas of the Madras rivers. This is shown by reference to the following table, in which are given the results of the profitable irrigation works:—

	Capital.	Receipts after meeting working expenses and interest at 4½ per cent.	Excess Revenue per cent.
	£	£	
Scinde Irrigation Works . .	667,704	132,103	19·66
East Jumna	231,743	47,946	20·68
West Jumna	432,764	84,010	19·42
Cauvery	116,072	108,923	81·30
Godavery	736,444	94,351	12·94
Kristnah	463,590	45,630	9·8
Ganges	2,826,479	42,808	1·51

With regard to the irrigation works which are not included in the above table, and on which a capital of no less than 10,197,869*l.* has been expended, the return yielded in 1875-76 was barely sufficient to meet the working expenses, and fell short by no less a sum than 421,859*l.* of the amount which was required to defray these expenses and the interest on the capital expended. This result is made still more unfavourable if the outlay on the Madras Irrigation Company's works is taken into account. These works, constructed with capital raised by a private company in England, were subsequently purchased by the Government, and on a capital expenditure of 1,372,000*l.* it appears that the net annual loss is 46,453*l.*

With regard to railways, which represent the other great branch of public works expenditure, the financial results which have up to the present time been obtained are no doubt in some respects more satisfactory, but as railways have now been constructed along the most important lines of communication, the returns which are yielded on the money expended on railways in the past ought not to be regarded as affording any evidence that similar returns will be obtained from capital which may be expended in the future. The construction of railways in India was first undertaken in 1846, and between that time and 1867 railways were made through the agency of private companies, who obtained from the Government a guarantee of interest, generally at 5 per cent., on the capital expended. It appears from the last official report on Indian railways, which brings the figures down to a year later than those contained in the report of the Public Works Committee, that the amount expended on the guaranteed railways up to March 1879 was 96,725,679*l.*

In 1867 it became apparent to the Government that the guarantee system afforded no adequate securities for economy. So long as private companies were insured somewhat more than the current rate of interest on whatever amount of capital they might expend, it is obvious that there could be no sufficient motive to restrain waste. It was accordingly decided to abandon the guarantee system, and from that time all new railways have been constructed by the Government. On these railways, which are known as the State railways, 21,291,076*l.* had been expended up to March 1879. It is scarcely possible to make any fair comparison between the financial results of the two systems, because, in the first place, the most profitable lines of communication were occupied by the guaranteed railways before the State railways were commenced, and, in the second place, a considerable portion of the capital which has been raised for these State railways has been expended on lines which are still in process of construction. It is shown in the report of the Public Works Committee that although there has recently been, on the average of years, an improvement in the returns of the guaranteed railways, yet in no single year except 1877-78 has the return on the aggregate expenditure on railways been sufficient to meet the interest on the capital expended. The entire loss on the guaranteed railways amounted up to 1877-78 to no less a sum than 22,437,307*l.* The comparatively favourable results which were obtained in that year are proved by the latest official reports to have been entirely exceptional, being favourably affected by the large quantities of grain which had to be taken to the famine districts in Southern India; between 1877-78 and 1878-79 there has been a very serious falling off in the returns from the guaranteed railways. The gross receipts have fallen nearly 12 per cent.; and as this falling off has been accompanied by an increase in the working expenses, there has been a still greater diminution in the net receipts, amounting to no less than 18 per cent. There has at the same time been an improvement in the returns from the State railways, as the net receipts from these have risen from 131,243*l.* to 195,787*l.* This increase is no doubt mainly due to the fact that nearly a thousand additional miles of railway were opened during the year. Assuming that a third or 7,000,000*l.* of the aggregate capital of 21,000,000*l.* raised for the State railways is being expended on lines which are not yet completed (and this is probably an excessive estimate), it appears from the figures just quoted that an outlay of 14,000,000*l.* only yields a return of 195,787*l.* It therefore follows that if, as is stated in the report of the Public Works Committee, the capital for the State railways has been borrowed at 4½ per cent. the lines which have been now completed do not yield a return sufficient to pay one third of the interest on the capital expended.

In view of such facts as those which have just been mentioned, it became impossible for the Government to resist the conclusion that, however great may be the advantages of extending railways and works of irrigation in India, the financial results of these undertakings were most uncertain, and were proved to be in many instances most disastrous. The continuance of the policy which had been for some time pursued of annually borrowing between 4,000,000*l.* and 5,000,000*l.* for public works would inevitably increase the deficit, which, as there was no surplus revenue, would have to be met either by an immediate increase of taxation, or by an increase of debt, which would sooner or later lead to the same result. The consequences produced by the new taxation which it has been found necessary to impose for the creation of a famine fund must have brought home to the Government with irresistible force that no misfortune which could happen to India could be greater than having to make her people bear the burden of increased taxation. It has therefore been most wisely resolved to lose no time in reducing the public works expenditure, and it has been ordered that in future the amount which shall be borrowed in any year for the construction of public works shall not exceed 2,500,000*l.* As it is strictly enjoined that the money shall be borrowed in India and not in England, it may be fairly concluded that the Government have at last recognised the political and financial disadvantage of adding to the indebtedness of India in England, and thus rendering it necessary each year to transmit a larger portion of the revenue of India in order to discharge her obligations to England.

This sudden curtailment of the public works expenditure cannot of course be regarded with unmixed satisfaction. Many most useful undertakings will undoubtedly be stopped; and it cannot be denied that many works which are not directly remunerative may produce such beneficial results that, if the financial condition of India were different from what it is, they might most properly be undertaken. But in her present situation the Government had only a choice of evils. No other alternative was open to them than either to continue an expenditure which would lead to increased taxation, or to adopt a policy which will only too certainly cause the stoppage of many useful works. Whilst fully acknowledging that the Government, in the course they have adopted, have chosen the less of these two evils, it is at the same time very important not to lose sight of the disadvantage that will result from this necessary reduction in the public works expenditure. Although I have for many years past had frequent occasion to call attention to the impolicy of raising large loans for the construction of public works, it is impossible to insist too strongly upon the fact that, whilst it may be most inexpedient to continue to carry out an extensive system of railways and irrigation schemes by loans, it may be most desirable to undertake them, if such a surplus of revenue can be obtained as will enable the works to be completed without increasing the taxation or adding to the debt of India. If any fresh inducement were required to make those who are responsible for the administration of the finances of India resolutely persist in a course of the most rigorous economy, it would be afforded by the fact that, until a large surplus is regularly obtained, many works will have to be suspended which would greatly promote the proper development of the resources of that country.

Enough has probably now been said to prove that

the time has arrived when, in order to restore the finances of India and prevent them drifting into hopeless embarrassment, it is absolutely essential that the policy of "rigid economy in every branch in the public service," which has been recently announced by the Government, should be carried out with promptitude and thoroughness. The necessity for this economy being fully admitted, it will naturally be asked, What are the measures which have been proposed by the Government to insure it? After what has been said with regard to public works, no detailed reference need be made to the contemplated reductions in this branch of the expenditure. During the present year the expenditure on public works is to be reduced from 4,599,000*l.*, its amount in 1878–79 to 3,500,000*l.*, and, as previously stated, the amount which is to be borrowed for public works in succeeding years is to be limited to 2,500,000*l.*, with the proviso that the entire amount required is to be raised in India. Considering the large public works establishments which exist in India, and the heavy sums which will be required to provide pensions for the engineers and others for whom, under the reduced scale of expenditure, no employment will be available, and also bearing in mind the serious loss that may be incurred in having suddenly to abandon works which are approaching completion, it may perhaps be fairly concluded that it would scarcely be prudent to make a larger immediate reduction in the public works expenditure than that which is now proposed. Unless, however, a decided improvement can be effected in the financial condition of India during the next few years, the Government will undoubtedly be compelled still further to reduce the outlay on public works.

In addition to these important reductions in the public works expenditure, the Government have given the most distinct pledges that no effort shall be spared to secure every possible retrenchment in all the other branches of civil administration. It is anticipated that an immediate saving of 250,000*l.* a year can thus be obtained, and it is evidently thought that a much larger saving can be secured, when sufficient time has elapsed to enable all the civil departments to be thoroughly overhauled. No one who has watched the steady and rapid growth in the cost of the civil administration since the government of India was transferred from the Company to the Crown, can doubt that there is an almost unlimited opportunity for effecting a most important saving if the government is conducted with greater care and thrift. It has been previously pointed out that the cost of administration, excluding expenditure on the army and public works, increased in the fifteen years from 1856 to 1871 from 14,964,867*l.* to 23,271,082*l.*, and this growth of expenditure has steadily continued up to the present time. It is shown in almost every item in the cost of administration. Thus, in 1856, the cost of printing and stationery was 128,197*l.*; in 1871, it was 233,675*l.*, and in the present year it is estimated at no less an amount than 490,000*l.* net. The advantage which would result from reducing this excessive outlay within proper limits is by no means to be measured by the amount of money which would be saved, for it will scarcely be denied that in the government of India administrative efficiency is often smothered in a mass of paper details. This remark admits of a very wide application, for there is good reason to believe that economy, instead of lessening, would in almost every instance greatly promote administrative efficiency in India. One of the chief defects in the present system of governing that country is the weakening of individual responsibility. Experience has again and again proved that no task is more hopeless than to attempt to fasten responsibility upon a particular department or individual for any mistake that may be committed, or for any waste that may result from laxity of control. Some years since barracks were erected in India at an enormous cost, and although it was afterwards found that in some instances they were so badly constructed as to be totally unfit for use, it has to this day remained impossible to discover to whom the blame ought to be attached. The subject was most carefully investigated by a select committee of the House of Commons, but it was soon seen that the members of that committee had a tangled skein before them, which no amount of patience or ingenuity could unravel. The responsibility in rapid succession was shifted from the Public Works Department to the various grades of engineers who were engaged in the work, and then again it was transferred from the engineers to the local contractors. The weakening of responsibility is always so much promoted by the undue multiplication of departments, that the rumoured decision of the Government to reduce the number of departments in India, many of which have been called into existence during the last few years, is to be welcomed not only on account of the important saving which will result from the abolition of many highly paid offices, but on account of the influence which it will undoubtedly exert upon the efficiency of administration.

The annual migration to Simla may be referred to as affording another example of the fact that, although economy may be the primary motive for adopting some particular measure, yet other consequences may be produced by it, which are at least as important as the pecuniary saving involved. It has been estimated that on the most moderate computation a saving of 10,000*l.* a year might be effected in connection with this migration. While, in the present state of the finances of India, it is imperatively incumbent on the Government to effect an economy comparatively so small as 10,000*l.*, such an amount altogether fails to represent the indirect loss which is caused to India by this transfer of the seat of government from Calcutta to Simla during the greater part of the year. The *personnel* of many of the most important offices is annually removed from Calcutta to Simla during seven months. As a fortnight is occupied both in going and returning, it follows that one-twelfth of the working year is lost. It has lately been well observed that no item in the Indian accounts "could be more safely or more advantageously cut down, if not swept away altogether. Up to about fifteen years ago the idea of removing all the departments to a summer capital seems never to have suggested itself. The Governor-General might, and often did, spend two or three months at one of the hill sanitaria, but never dreamt of taking with him the whole apparatus of government. . . . Such public opinion and independent criticism as there are in India are to be found only in the Presidency towns, and it is no light evil that the Government should be out of the reach of the wholesome effect of these for over half the year. Moreover, Simla is situated in a remote and inaccessible corner of the Empire, and the Government might be easily cut off for days from all communication with the rest of the country. If, however, the Government cannot make up its mind to give up this luxury, it may fairly be asked whether the officers whose work lies for five months in Calcutta and seven in Simla—in other words, who enjoy an almost perfect climate for the entire year—should receive salaries and have furlough privileges which were originally fixed with the view of tempting equally good men to spend their whole time in the plains."[1]

As already stated, the Government, with the view of securing economy, have undertaken that all branches of expenditure shall be most carefully scrutinised. It will no doubt be found that by abolishing many unnecessary offices a considerable saving may be effected, but in order to make such retrenchment as is rendered absolutely necessary by the present financial condition of India, it will be essential that something more shall be done. The

[1] See Calcutta correspondent of the *Times*, July 7, 1879.

entire system on which the government of India has been conducted must be changed. The illusion is only just beginning to pass away that India is an extremely wealthy country. Misled by certain signs of barbaric riches, people have too generally supposed that India could afford to have her government carried on upon a lavish scale. There is probably no country in which official salaries range so high, and this remark holds true not only with regard to those who are employed in the public service in India, but also with regard to many of the salaries which are paid at the India Office in London. One who holds a high position in the English Civil Service informs me that he has lately had occasion to make a comparison between the rates of pay in the English and Indian services, and that he finds that in numerous instances, for precisely the same work done in England, a poor country like India pays 20 or 30 per cent. more than is paid by England with all her wealth. In determining at what amount official salaries should be fixed, it is not sufficient merely to consider whether a particular individual is overpaid. The financial circumstances of the country must also be most carefully taken into account. The worst of all things for a state as well as for an individual is, by living beyond its means, to burden itself with a load of debt. If a comparison is made between the financial resources of England and India, it will be found almost impossible to convey an adequate idea of the poverty of the latter country. In India, with a population of more than 200,000,000, a net revenue is raised of less than 38,000,000*l.* A much larger revenue than this is raised in England by taxes imposed on articles of general consumption; but in India the mass of the people are in a condition of such deplorable poverty, many of them earning only 3*d.* a day, that with the exception of salt, which is already heavily taxed, they consume scarcely an article on which a duty can be imposed, and consequently it is found that taxation in India has reached almost its extreme limits. An expenditure which may be perfectly suited to England may be altogether beyond the means of India; and if India cannot afford to pay some of those who are now receiving seven or eight thousand a year, it is far better that she should get others to do the work for a smaller remuneration than incur debt and thus ultimately be driven to bear fresh burdens of taxation.

It will unfortunately only too surely happen that a policy of retrenchment cannot be carried out without causing much loss and suffering to individuals. If, for instance, the public works expenditure is reduced by one half, many thousands of labourers who are now employed by the Government will have to be dismissed. The Indian newspapers already contain accounts of the suffering which is thus caused by the curtailment of the outlay on public works. Not the least of the many evils that result from extravagance is that, when the inevitable time arrives for retrenchment, many old servants have to be dismissed, and many, through no fault of their own, are deprived of employment to which they have been long accustomed. At such a time it is of the first importance that a Government should mete out even-handed justice, and that retrenchment should not fall upon the poor alone, and leave the wealthy and the influential untouched. The difficulties which must always be encountered by a Government in carrying out a policy of economy are sure to be most formidable; but the Government of India will find that the task which they have undertaken is rendered much more easy if they are able to give proofs that, in order to secure a reduction of expenditure, they do not shrink from encountering the opposition of those whose influence will enable them to make their complaints heard.

In attempting to describe the advantages which will be produced by this new policy of economy to which the Indian Government is now pledged, it is hardly possible to lay too much stress upon the fact that one of the chief agencies on which reliance seems to be placed is to secure a more economical administration by a larger employment of natives in the public service. The question is alike important whether regarded in its political or its financial aspects. There can be no surer way of attaching the people of India to our rule than to place within their reach an education which will fit them for the public service, and then freely to throw open to them all positions which they are qualified to fill. In spite of repeated pledges that no unnecessary barriers should be placed in the way of the natives obtaining admission to the public service, it is now officially acknowledged that the efforts to give these pledges practical effect have been "spasmodic, unsystematic, and altogether incomprehensible to the mass of the native population, while the great increase which has taken place in the number of Europeans in some branches of the public service, and various other acts, may have seemed to them to be in partial violation of this policy. It cannot be denied that, whatever may have been the intentions of successive Secretaries of State, very little progress has been made in giving effect to it."[1] As I have had occasion to express strong dissent from many acts of the present Viceroy, I more gladly take this opportunity of bearing testimony to the efforts which he is understood to have made during the whole time

[1] See the Budget Speech of Mr. Stanhope, House of Commons, May 22, 1879.

he has been in India to secure a larger employment of natives in the public service. In pursuing this course it will, I believe, be subsequently proved that Lord Lytton has acted with not less wisdom than justice. Indications, however, are not wanting that, in carrying out this policy, the Government will be attacked from two opposite quarters. No sooner was the announcement made that, in order to admit natives to some of the higher offices, the number of appointments in the covenanted service thrown open to competition in England would be diminished, than the course which the Government intended to adopt was severely criticised. All the old and well-known objections were brought forward. It was alleged that the natives were defective in physique, and that they were morally unfit to have entrusted to them the higher offices of the State. It is only reasonable to suppose that such objections as these have been carefully considered both by the Viceroy and the Secretary of State before they came to their recent decision, and in arriving at it it is easy to show that they are supported by those whose intimate knowledge of India has qualified them to speak with great authority on this subject. Selecting a few from many similar expressions of opinion that might be quoted, General Sir George Jacob, formerly Special Political Commissioner, Southern Mahratta country, saïd : "During the last thirty years that I have been at the head of a province or provinces, I have made it a rule to select men for employ under me from the different colleges and schools of the Presidency, both Mahometan and Hindu, and there are numbers who have been so selected who are now filling high and responsible appointments in the different parts of Western India. The accounts that have reached me of them since my return to England bear testimony to their usefulness and trustworthiness." After saying that only one had failed, he continued: "I certainly should not have expected so large a proportion of good men and true even from the educated classes of my own country." Sir Bartle Frere, writing in 1868, when he was Governor of Bombay, said: "We have at this moment in the educated youth of Western India, as far as intellectual and moral training can secure it, an excellent raw material for manning every branch of the public service." The present Governor of Bombay, Sir Richard Temple, who has also held important positions in Bengal, bears testimony to the capacity possessed by some of the natives for the highest administrative work. He says that during our supremacy in India there have been in the native States "good ministers, really capital administrators, who have adorned the service to which they belong: such as Purnea of Mysore, the Tantia Jogh of Indore, in the past, and Sir Sala Jung of Hyderabad, Sir Dinker Rao of Gwalior, Sir T. Madhava Rao of Travancore, in the present." In a report which the Government of India published a few years since on Sir T. Madhava Rao's administration of Travancore, it is stated that "he found Travancore, when he went there in 1849, in the lowest stage of degradation; he has left it a model State." Everything was in a condition of the most utter disorder; the treasury was exhausted; the pay of the police and other public servants was so much in arrear that they compensated themselves by the most irregular exactions. Sir Madhava Rao, by the exercise of the greatest care and thrift, was able to place the finances of Travancore in a thoroughly sound position; a considerable surplus was secured, large sums were spent on education and in the construction of public works, the salaries of the officials were regularly paid, the people were not harassed by taxes unsuited to them, but his intimate knowledge of their tastes and their habits enabled him to effect all these great reforms with the minimum of inconvenience to the people. If any other proof were wanted of the great advantage that would result from more largely employing natives who are capable of rendering important service to the Government, it would be afforded by the fact that almost all the public works in India have in recent years been constructed by English engineers, and yet, as previously shown, by far the most successful schemes of irrigation are those which were designed by natives, who possessed a knowledge of the climatic conditions of the country which can be very rarely acquired by a foreigner. This success of the native works is so remarkable that when Lord Salisbury was Secretary of State he went so far as to declare that the only schemes of irrigation which showed the desirable result of a clean balance-sheet were those of native origin.

As previously indicated, the extended employment of natives in the public service ought not to be simply considered as a measure of justice and of improved administration. The Government wisely consider that by the adoption of this policy, it will be possible to effect a very important reduction in expenditure. It is, however, evident that claims may be put forward by the people of India themselves, which, if conceded, would prevent any direct pecuniary gain being secured from the increased employment of natives in the public service. It is often contended by influential representatives of native opinion that there should be no difference in the remuneration of natives and Europeans respectively for the same work. The salary of a European official in India should, however, be considered as composed of two elements: one part of the pay which he receives remunerates him for the actual work which he does, and the other compensates him for leaving his country, and for various expenses to which he is subjected, such, for instance, as having to send his children to Europe to be educated. A native, therefore, not being subject to these disadvantages, would really receive much higher remuneration than a European if he were paid the same salary. One simple principle should regulate the official pay both of natives and of Europeans. The Government, being trustees of the public revenue, are not justified in spending one shilling of this revenue unnecessarily, and consequently they are bound not to pay more for any work which may require to be done than is sufficient to secure the services of those who are competent to perform it. If a qualified native is willing to accept 1,000*l.* a year where it would be requisite to give an equally competent European 2,000*l.* a year, a strong argument is afforded, not for making an unnecessary addition of 1,000*l.* a year to the salary of the native, but for saving this amount by employing him instead of the European.

Although much may be undoubtedly done to improve the financial position of India by carrying out a policy of strict retrenchment in all departments of civil administration, yet it will scarcely be denied that, in order to effect the saving which is needed, chief reliance must be placed on largely diminishing the present cost of the Indian army. It appears, from the latest official statement,[1] that the net cost of the Indian army for the present year is estimated at 17,375,000*l.* A considerable portion of the cost of the late Afghan war will have to be borne during the present year; but as, at the time when the military expenditure was estimated at 17,375,000*l.*, peace had been restored, and no renewal of hostilities was anticipated, it may be only too certainly concluded that the military expenditure for the present year will greatly exceed the amount stated. Even in the time of peace the cost of the army has of late years shown a tendency to increase, for in 1877, when there was no war, Sir John Strachey laid special stress upon the fact that in a single year there had been an increase of no less than 1,000,000*l.* in military expenditure. It is evident that, if decided measures are not at once taken, the military expenditure will soon absorb one half of the entire net revenue of India. It would be difficult for any country, and it is impossible for one so poor as India, to bear such a drain on her resources. The Government

[1] See Budget Speech of Sir John Strachey, Calcutta, March, 1879.

seem at length fully to have recognised the necessity of immediately adopting measures to reduce this expenditure. A commission, with Sir Ashley Eden, the present Lieutenant-Governor of Bengal, as its president, has been appointed in India, "with a view to assist Government in determining what share of the unavoidable reductions in public expenditure can be borne by the military charges without injury to the general efficiency of the army, and in what manner such savings can best be effected." Simultaneously a small commission has been appointed in England to investigate the home army charges which are borne by India, especially those connected with the cost of recruits. This commission consists of Lord Northbrook, Sir Thomas Seccombe, who for many years ably discharged the duties of Financial Secretary at the India Office, and Mr. Knox, Deputy Accountant-General at the War Office, who has deservedly gained the confidence of successive Secretaries of State for War. It may be anticipated that much good will result from these inquiries, and that many suggestions will be made which, if adopted, will lead to a considerable reduction of expenditure. Thus it can hardly be doubted that the Commission in India will recommend the abolition of the offices of Commander-in-Chief at Bombay and Madras, with a considerable portion of their costly and unnecessary staff. Public opinion in India is almost unanimously in favour of this change, and it was long since strongly advocated by some of the highest authorities, such as Lord Sandhurst and Sir Henry Durand, not only on the ground of economy, but also as likely to add to the efficiency of the army. The experience of the recent Afghan war must enforce upon the Commission the conclusion that the present commissariat system is alike costly and defective. The large amount which India has annually to spend in non-effective army charges cannot fail to be a prominent subject in any inquiry which has for its object the reduction of the military expenditure of that country. The sum which India has annually to pay in pensions is steadily increasing, and many of these pensions, earned after a comparatively short period of service, are received by those who are still capable of doing useful work for the State. Thus, in an account of the Indian army lately published, it is stated that "at the present moment there are thousands of soldiers who have completed little over fifteen years' service in India in receipt of pensions for life." If some kind of civil employment in India were given to these men, the army would become more popular, and the burden of the pension establishment be sensibly lightened. The question of the non-effective charges presents itself in a still more serious aspect when the pensions and furlough allowances received by officers in the Indian army are considered. It was stated before the Indian Finance Committee in 1872 by Sir Thomas Pears, then Military Secretary at the India Office, that India was at that time annually paying no less than 1,600,000*l.* to officers in the form of pensions and furlough allowances, and he showed that about one-fourth of the entire number of officers of the Indian army, who are wholly maintained by India, were not in India, but in England. When such questions as these are investigated, I believe the Commissions which have just been appointed, will arrive at the conclusion that in order to effect any important reduction in the military expenditure of India, it will not be sufficient simply to deal with details, but it will be necessary to introduce fundamental changes into the system on which the present Indian army is based. With regard to the army, a partnership has been established between England and India, and as one of these countries is extremely rich, and the other extremely poor, much of the same incongruity and many of the same inconveniences arise as if two individuals were to join in housekeeping, one of whom had 20,000*l.* a year, and the other only

1,000*l.* An expenditure which may be quite appropriate to the one whose income is 20,000*l.* would bring nothing but embarrassment to the one whose income is only 1,000*l.* The money which is expended may be judiciously laid out, but if the man with the smaller income finds that he is gradually becoming embarrassed with debt because he has to live beyond his means, it is no compensation to him to be told that he is only called on to contribute his proper share of the expenses. His position would be the more intolerable if he were treated as India was as regards her army, and, after having been compelled against his wish to join the partnership, he is forced to continue it whether he desires to do so or not. In 1861 the English and Indian armies were amalgamated in direct opposition to the strongly-expressed remonstrances of Lord Canning, who was then Viceroy, and of almost every Indian statesman of authority and experience. The Council of the Secretary of State unanimously objected to it, but they were informed that although they could, of course, exercise their right of protest, it would be time wasted, for the amalgamation of the two armies had been made a Cabinet question, and was an accomplished fact.

The description just given of the consequences which may occur if two individuals share the cost of joint housekeeping, fails fully to indicate the position of India with regard to army expenditure. Not only has she been compelled to enter into partnership with England, but, the partnership having been once established, she is obliged to contribute her share towards the expenses of many costly arrangements, as to the adoption of which she was not even consulted. Thus, a few years since, the system of short service was introduced. Under the arrangement which previously prevailed, a man was enlisted for twenty-one years, during twelve of which he served with the colours. Now, the enlistment is for twelve years; there is only six years' service with the colours; for the remaining six he passes into the reserve. Whatever may be urged in favour of this new arrangement, it is obvious that short service may produce very different consequences to India and England respectively. For instance, the cost of transporting troops from England to India is an important item in the military expenditure of the latter country, and it is evident that the shorter the term of service, the more frequently will troops have to be sent from England to India, and back again from India to England, with the result of very materially adding to the charge for transport. This charge has to be borne entirely by India, and does not in the slightest degree affect England. Again, it may very possibly happen that six years' service in England may be sufficient to enable a man to pass into the reserve as a thoroughly trained soldier; if, however, the great majority of those who have completed six years' service in India do not remain there, but return to England, India will have scarcely any reserve of well-trained troops, and the larger part of her European forces will consist of young soldiers, who have not been long enough in the country to become either properly trained or properly acclimatised. From these and other considerations which might be mentioned, it is at once evident that although the system of short service may be a good arrangement for England, it does not necessarily follow that the system is calculated to promote either the economy or the efficiency of the military organisation of India. The interests of India, however, in this matter were so entirely ignored or lost sight of by the English Government that it appears from official evidence given before a committee of the House of Commons, that there is no record to show that when the short service system was adopted, those who were responsible for the government of India were even consulted on the subject.[1]

[1] See evidence given by Sir Thomas Pears, late Secretary of the Military Department at the Indian Office, before the East India Finance Committee, 1874, p. 53.

When it is proved, as it repeatedly has been before parliamentary and departmental committees, that India has at the present time to pay at least twice as much for her recruits as she would have to pay if she could obtain them for herself, and when it is pointed out how costly to her in various other ways is the army partnership which has been established between her and England, it is usually urged that the general interests of England and the rest of the Empire render the maintenance of this partnership necessary. Thus it is said, "If England and India both competed in the English labour market for recruits, various inconveniences might arise." In the days of the Company, India had a European army of her own, and although she obtained her recruits at an extremely cheap rate, yet service in the Company's European army was always eagerly sought after. India, if she were again permitted to recruit for herself, might make service in her army so attractive, that, to the disadvantage of England, she would draw away some of the best recruits. But, if for any such reasons as these, it is necessary to make India compulsorily share in the costly military organisation of England, the greatest care should be taken not to throw upon her any charge which she would not have to bear if she were allowed to obtain recruits on her own terms, and make her own arrangements with the officers she employed. There is too much ground for the suspicion that an exactly opposite course is now often followed, for facts may be mentioned which seem to show that the large amount which India in some instances pays, diminishes the amount which England would otherwise have to give for services which she receives. Thus, before a Committee of the House of Commons which sat in 1877, it was stated that although the pay of the private soldier and the non-commissioned officer is the same in India as in England, yet the commissioned officers are much more highly paid when serving in the former country than in the latter. An official return was laid before the Committee by which it was shown that the pay of officers of the higher ranks is "at least three times as much in India as in England."[1] The unhealthiness of the Indian climate cannot be pleaded as a sufficient reason why this higher rate of pay should be given to officers of the English army serving in India; the climate is not worse for them than it is for the private soldier or the non-commissioned officer, and their pay is the same in India as in England. India is not a worse place for an English officer to live in than Sierra Leone or Canton: if he is stationed

[1] See Report of the Army (Royal Artillery and Engineer Officers') Arrears of Pay Committee, 1877, p. 72.

at these places his pay is provided by the English taxpayer, and the amount he receives is almost precisely the same as if he were serving in England. It may no doubt be contended that the aggregate remuneration which an officer of the British army receives for service in England and in India admits of no reduction, and that, as he is certainly not overpaid, if he were to receive less in India it would be necessary to give him more in England; but even if this were fully admitted, it would only supply one more unanswerable argument to show that, when the respective financial interests of England and India are in question, sufficient care is not taken to give adequate protection to India.

Nothing would be more unwise than to underrate the difficulties which will have to be encountered by any Government that is determined to effect such reductions in Indian expenditure as those which have here been indicated. It will only too certainly be found that it is impossible to advance a single step in the path of economy without an attempt being made to bar the way by those who wish to maintain the particular item of expenditure which it is proposed to touch. If the Government should give proof that they are determined to pursue a policy of rigorous retrenchment with unflinching courage, they have a right to expect that they shall be generously and cordially supported by every one who is interested in the future of India. The work cannot be done by the Government alone. It will be necessary that they shall be aided both by Parliament and by public opinion in this country. Hitherto it has unfortunately too frequently happened that the influence of the House of Commons has, with regard to the expenditure of Indian money, been on the side of extravagance. But Parliament reflects the opinion of the constituencies, and the humblest elector may help on the work which is to be done, if, awakening to the responsibility which every Englishman owes to the great dependency we have to govern, he makes it clear that it is his wish that no charge which ought in justice to be borne by England should be thrown upon India, and that the spending of Indian money should be watched with at least as much care as the spending of English money. It was once well said that in politics as in other affairs the difficulty of doing a particular thing is not unfrequently the measure of the good which its accomplishment will secure. This is certainly true with regard to the reform of the finances of India. Few tasks can be more difficult, but no labour will yield a richer harvest of results. Two paths are now before the Indian Government: the one will lead to augmented indebtedness, increased taxation, and growing discontent; the other, if resolutely followed, will enable debt to be diminished, taxation to be reduced, and will cause our rule in India to rest on its only sure foundation—the contentment and happiness of the people. If three or four millions in the annual expenditure of India can be saved, the licence tax could be repealed, the salt duty reduced to a uniform rate of two rupees per maund, and many useful works which have now to be suspended could be resumed without incurring fresh indebtedness. When it is remembered that such results as these may be effected by a policy of retrenchment, we may with confidence indulge the hope that the work, having been undertaken, will not be abandoned until it has been accomplished.

APPENDIX.

APPENDIX.

THE AMENDMENT OF THE TRADES LICENCE-TAX, AND THE RELINQUISHMENT OF THE FAMINE FUND.

In the last Essay, reference was made to the many gratifying indications afforded by recent events that, with the general recognition of the true financial condition of India, a new spirit would in future be likely to control the administration of the finances of that country. During the few months which have elapsed since this opinion was expressed many circumstances have occurred which afford additional proof that reforms which before seemed to be unattainable will now be readily conceded. Thus, in directing attention to the trades' licence-tax and to the famine fund, I have had frequent occasion to refer to the extremely oppressive character of the tax as it affected the very poor, to the great inequality in its incidence, and to the confusion which was introduced into Indian finance by the nominal maintenance of a famine fund, after the revenue yielded by the taxes from which this fund was created had been devoted to objects in no way connected with the relief of famine. From the first moment that the trades' licence-tax was imposed, public opinion in England and in India condemned with remarkable unanimity the injustice of a tax which, while it was levied from petty traders and handicraftsmen whose incomes were only four shillings a week, left altogether untouched the highly-paid officials, all military officers, and all professional men. Petitions most numerously and influentially signed by all classes of natives in India were presented in both Houses of Parliament against the continuance of these inequalities in the tax, and on several occasions the prayer of these petitions was supported by those who could speak with most authority and weight on a question of taxation. Striking instances were given of the abuses and difficulties inseparably associated with the assessment and levying of direct taxation imposed upon the very poor in such a country as India; but for a long time the Government, both in England and in India, appeared to be deaf to all remonstrance.

Within the last few weeks, however, a change, as remarkable as it is satisfactory, has taken place in the attitude which had hitherto been officially assumed with regard to the licence-tax. On the

14th of November, the Finance Minister, Sir John Strachey, brought forward, at a meeting of the Legislative Council of the Viceroy, a Bill for the amendment of this tax, which, though it left some inequalities unredressed, introduced many important improvements. It will be at once seen from a brief description of the provisions of the Bill that it fully recognised the justice of the most serious objections which had been urged against the tax. As previously stated, only those traders whose incomes were less than 100 rupees a year were exempted from the tax; by the Bill the limit of exemption was raised from 100 rupees to 250 rupees. It is supposed that the number of persons to whom relief would thus be given would not be less than a million. The Bill effected another not less important change, by subjecting to a uniform tax of 1½ per cent. the incomes derived from professions, and the salaries of all those in Government and other employment. The previous exemption of many who were among the wealthiest people in India had naturally provoked strong and widespread discontent. It was calculated that the proposed exemption of incomes below 250 rupees a year would cause a loss to the revenue of about 240,000*l.*, and that this would be approximately made good by the additional revenue yielded by the new classes of incomes to be brought within the operation of the tax. Although the tax would thus undoubtedly have been placed on a much fairer basis, yet the Bill created some new anomalies and left many inequalities unredressed. Thus, "it is proposed to exempt from liability to the tax the military servants of Government, not in civil employment, whose pay and allowances do not exceed 500 rupees per mensem, or 6,000 rupees per annum;" and for all other salaried persons "it is proposed to make 100 rupees per mensem, or 1,200 rupees per annum, the lower limit of taxable income." It is difficult to suggest any valid reasons in support of an arrangement which would impose taxation on a petty trader whose income is only 250 rupees, and exempt from taxation persons in receipt of salaries five times as large, and military officers with incomes twenty-four times as large. These exemptions excited much hostile criticism in India when the Bill was introduced, and it was generally felt that too small a sum had been taken in fixing the lower limit of taxation at 250 rupees. The Indian Government very wisely showed an inclination to yield to these expressions of public opinion, and accordingly, on the 24th of December, Sir John Strachey brought forward the Licence-Tax Bill in an amended form, and proposed at a meeting of the Legislative Council that the Bill should be referred to a Select Committee, with the object of passing it after the introduction of the next Indian Budget. The full details of these amendments have not yet been published.

It appears, however, that one important change is to be effected, for the limit of exemption is to be raised from 250 to 500 rupees. It is also proposed that the maximum amount to be taken from any person who is not an official should be 800 rupees, but that a tax of 1½ per cent. should be imposed on official salaries without limitation. It is not stated, in the accounts which have reached England of the Bill in its new form, whether or not military officers whose pay and allowances are less than 6,000 rupees a year, and persons in receipt of salaries of less than 1,200 rupees a year, are still to be exempted from the tax. Although it seems impossible to defend the continuance of these exemptions, yet enough has been said to show that the tax in its new form will bear a striking contrast to the tax as it was originally, and is still, imposed. Many of the most glaring inequalities in its incidence will be removed, and so much relief will be afforded to the very poor by raising the limit of exemption from incomes of 100 to 500 rupees, that it is estimated that no less than 1,750,000 persons who now pay the tax will in future be freed from all liability to contribute to it. This important measure of relief will not involve any serious sacrifice of revenue, for it is officially calculated that the tax in its new form will produce only 100,000*l.* less than it now yields. It may be hoped that the experience which has been derived from the licence-tax since it has been in operation will not be lost on future Indian Governments. It has been shown by what has occurred, that nothing can politically be more unwise and financially more inexpedient than to impose direct taxation in India upon the possessors of very small incomes. The difficulty of equitably assessing and collecting direct taxation when it reaches the very poor in such a country is so great, and the revenue which is yielded is so trifling, that it may be fairly said that the maximum of inconvenience is caused in order to secure a minimum of revenue.

By the Bill for the amendment of the licence-tax it is proposed to carry out another change of much importance. It will be remembered that this tax, with others, was originally imposed with the object of creating a famine fund. In the preamble of the Act by which the licence-tax is now levied, it is stated that these taxes were imposed with the object of effecting "a permanent increase of the revenue, in order to provide means for defraying the public expenditure from time to time incurred, and to be incurred, for the relief and prevention of famine in British India." In the preamble of the new Bill all reference to the relief of famine is omitted. I think there will be general concurrence with the opinion expressed by Sir John Strachey, that the retention of these words would "undoubtedly serve to create misapprehension." I have already adduced reasons which seem to me to show that, at a time when it is necessary for the Indian Government to raise loans both in England and in India, the employment of any language which would encourage the idea that a separate fund had been called into existence for the relief of famine, could produce no other result except to introduce unnecessary confusion into Indian finance. It is in every respect far better to adopt the course which is now about to be taken by the Indian Government, and to treat the licence-tax as an impost levied in order to obtain the additional revenue which was required, when, in consequence of the frequent occurrence of famine, the decision was arrived at that the relief of famine was an ordinary charge, for which it was just as incumbent to make provision as it is for "proper courts of justice, police, education, and so forth." [1]

[1] See speech of Sir John Strachey in introducing the amended Licence-tax Bill.

Although the famine fund has, for the reasons just stated, been wisely relinquished, yet it cannot be too carefully borne in mind that the obligation to make provision for the relief of famine, in those years when there are no famines, remains precisely the same as it was before. As the Government have arrived at the conclusion that the amount which ought to be thus appropriated is about 1,500,000*l.* a year, it is manifest that in years when there are no famines a surplus of at least this amount ought to be regularly secured. There now seems to be every reason to hope that the present financial year, which ends on the 31st of March next, will in many respects afford a gratifying contrast to those which have immediately preceded it. The seasons have been favourable, and the harvests have been good; arrears of land revenue, which the people had before been too poor to pay, are now beginning to come in; and it is expected that the land revenue will yield about 350,000*l.* more than was estimated. During the time that large districts of India were afflicted with famine the people were obliged to lessen their consumption even of an article so necessary to life as salt. With the return of better times the consumption of salt is increasing, and the salt revenue is likely to yield 200,000*l.* more than was estimated. Although little more than eight months have elapsed since the

Government, at the time of the discussion of the last Indian Budget in the House of Commons, first announced their determination that greater economy should be introduced into the administration of Indian finance, and that a policy of rigorous retrenchment should be carried out in every branch of expenditure, yet, short as the time has been, it has been long enough to show how important are the results which may be achieved if such a policy is resolutely and persistently pursued. This improvement, however, in the financial condition of India does not render vigilance and caution in the slightest degree less necessary. If there is not constant watchfulness, nothing will be more easy than to glide back into the old ways of carelessness and extravagance, and although the seasons may this year be propitious, the experience of the past should ever be present to remind us that a period of plenty may be succeeded by years of famine, and that it is the first maxim of prudent and wise finance to make provision in prosperous days to meet the difficulties of adverse times.

LONDON:
R. CLAY, SONS, AND TAYLOR, PRINTERS,
BREAD STREET HILL, E.C.

PRACTICAL POLITICS:

(*Issued by the National Liberal Federation.*)

No. I.—THE TENANT FARMER; LAND LAWS, AND LANDLORDS. By JAMES HOWARD. 8vo. 1*s.*

No. II.—FOREIGN POLICY. By M. E. GRANT DUFF, M.P. 8vo. 1*s.*

No. III.—FREEDOM OF LAND. By G. SHAW LEFEVRE, M.P. 8vo. 2*s.* 6*d.*

Others to follow.

BY PROFESSOR JEVONS, F.R.S.

THE THEORY OF POLITICAL ECONOMY. New Edition, revised with new Preface, &c. 8vo. 10*s.* 6*d.*

PRIMER OF POLITICAL ECONOMY. 18mo. 1*s.*

BY W. T. THORNTON, C.B.

ON LABOUR: its Wrongful Claims and Rightful Dues: Actual Present and Possible Future. Second Edition. 8vo. 14*s.*

A PLEA FOR PEASANT PROPRIETORS: with the Outlines of a Plan for their Establishment in Ireland. New Edition. Crown 8vo. 7*s.* 6*d.*

INDIAN PUBLIC WORKS AND OTHER COGNATE INDIAN TOPICS. Crown 8vo. 8*s.* 6*d.*

BY THE RIGHT HON. JOHN BRIGHT, M.P.

PUBLIC ADDRESSES. Edited by J. E. THOROLD ROGERS. 8vo. 14*s.*

SPEECHES ON QUESTIONS OF PUBLIC POLICY. Edited by J. E. THOROLD ROGERS. Author's Popular Edition. Crown 8vo. 3*s.* 6*d.*
Library Edition. 2 vols. 8vo. with Portrait, 25*s.*

RICHARD COBDEN'S SPEECHES ON QUESTIONS OF PUBLIC POLICY. Edited by the Right Hon. JOHN BRIGHT, M.P., and J. E. THOROLD ROGERS. Cheaper Edition. Crown 8vo. 3*s.* 6*d.*

COBDEN AND POLITICAL OPINION. By J. E. THOROLD ROGERS. 8vo. 10*s.* 6*d.*

MESSRS. MACMILLAN AND CO.'S PUBLICATIONS.

BY M. E. GRANT DUFF, M.P.

MISCELLANIES, POLITICAL AND LITERARY.

8vo. 10*s.* 6*d.*

NOTES OF AN INDIAN JOURNEY. 8vo. 10*s.* 6*d.*

BY SIR JOHN LUBBOCK, M.P., F.R.S., &c.

POLITICAL AND EDUCATIONAL ADDRESSES.

8vo. 8*s.* 6*d.*

PRIMITIVE PROPERTY. By M. DE LAVELEYE.

Translated by G. R. MARRIOTT, LL.B. With an Introduction by T. E. CLIFFE-LESLIE, LL.B. 8vo. 12*s.*

"It is almost impossible to over-estimate the value of the well-digested knowledge which it contains; it is one of the most learned books that have been contributed to the historical department of the literature of economic science."—*Athenæum.*

VILLAGE POLITICS: Addresses and Sermons on

the Labour Question. By C. W. STUBBS, M.A., Vicar of Granborough, Bucks. Extra fcap. 8vo. 3*s.* 6*d.*

"It is dedicated to the farm labourers of England .... and if it is read as it deserves to be, will do more to put their case before the country than any previous publication we know of."—*Academy.*

THE HOUSE OF COMMONS: Illustrations of its

History and Practice. By R. F. D. PALGRAVE, Clerk Assistant of the House of Commons. New Edition. Crown 8vo. 2*s.* 6*d.*

CYPRUS AS I SAW IT IN 1879. By SIR

SAMUEL W. BAKER, F.R.S., &c., Author of "Ismailïa," "The Albert Nyanza," &c. 8vo., with Frontispiece, 12*s.* 6*d.*

"We strongly advise all politicians to try and read at once the book."—*Spectator.*

"This work may be viewed under two distinct aspects—its importance as a contribution to scientific and political knowledge, and its interest as a book of travel and adventure. It is equally good from both points .... The book is a charming one, and the greatest praise that can be bestowed on it is to say that it is in every way worthy of its author."—*Morning Post.*

"The book may safely be pronounced to be by far the most valuable contribution that has yet appeared towards enabling us to form an impartial estimate of the present condition and future prospects of our new acquisition."—*Academy.*

CYPRUS; its History, its Present Resources, and

Future Prospects. By R. HAMILTON LANG, late H.M.'s Consul for the Island of Cyprus. With Four Maps and Two Illustrations. 8vo. 14*s.*

"The fair and impartial account of her past and present to be found in these pages has an undoubted claim on the attention of all intelligent readers."—*Morning Post.*

MACMILLAN AND CO., LONDON,

BEDFORD STREET, STRAND, LONDON, W.C.
August, 1879.

MACMILLAN & CO.'S CATALOGUE of Works in the Departments of History, Biography, Travels, Critical and Literary Essays, Politics, Political and Social Economy, Law, etc.; and Works connected with Language.

HISTORY, BIOGRAPHY, TRAVELS, &c.

Albemarle.—FIFTY YEARS OF MY LIFE. By GEORGE THOMAS, Earl of Albemarle. With Steel Portrait of the first Earl of Albemarle, engraved by JEENS. Third and Cheaper Edition. Crown 8vo. 7*s*. 6*d*.

"*The book is one of the most amusing of its class. . . . These reminiscences have the charm and flavour of personal experience, and they bring us into direct contact with the persons they describe.*"—EDINBURGH REVIEW.

Anderson.—MANDALAY TO MOMIEN; a Narrative of the Two Expeditions to Western China, of 1868 and 1875, under Colonel E. B. Sladen and Colonel Horace Browne. By Dr. ANDERSON, F.R.S.E., Medical and Scientific Officer to the Expeditions. With numerous Maps and Illustrations. 8vo. 21*s*.

"*A handsome, well-timed, entertaining, and instructive volume.*"—ACADEMY.

"*A pleasant, useful, carefully-written, and important work.*"—ATHENÆUM.

Appleton.—Works by T. G. APPLETON :—

A NILE JOURNAL. Illustrated by EUGENE BENSON. Crown 8vo. 6*s*.

SYRIAN SUNSHINE. Crown 8vo. 6*s*.

Arnold.—ESSAYS IN CRITICISM. By MATTHEW ARNOLD. New Edition, Revised and Enlarged. Crown 8vo. 9*s*.

Atkinson.—AN ART TOUR TO NORTHERN CAPITALS OF EUROPE, including Descriptions of the Towns, the Museums, and other Art Treasures of Copenhagen, Christiania, Stockholm,

Abo, Helsingfors, Wiborg, St. Petersburg, Moscow, and Kief. By J. BEAVINGTON ATKINSON. 8vo. 12*s.*

"*Although the main purpose of the book is strictly kept in view, and we never forget for long that we are travelling with a student and connoisseur, Mr. Atkinson gives variety to his narrative by glimpses of scenery and brief allusions to history and manners which are always welcome when they occur, and are never wordy or overdone. We have seldom met with a book in which what is principal and what is accessory have been kept in better proportion to each other.*"—SATURDAY REVIEW.

Bailey.—THE SUCCESSION TO THE ENGLISH CROWN. A Historical Sketch. By A. BAILEY, M.A., Barrister-at-Law. Crown 8vo. 7*s.* 6*d.*

Baker (Sir Samuel W.)—Works by Sir SAMUEL BAKER, Pacha, M.A., F.R.G.S.:—

ISMAILIA: A Narrative of the Expedition to Central Africa for the Suppression of the Slave Trade, organised by Ismail, Khedive of Egypt. With Portraits, Map, and fifty full-page Illustrations by ZWECKER and DURAND. New and Cheaper Edition. With New Preface. Crown 8vo. 6*s.*

"*A book which will be read with very great interest.*"—TIMES. "*Well written and full of remarkable adventures.*"—PALL MALL GAZETTE. "*Adds another thrilling chapter to the history of African adventure.*"—DAILY NEWS. "*Reads more like a romance . . . . incomparably more entertaining than books of African travel usually are.*"—MORNING POST.

THE ALBERT N'YANZA Great Basin of the Nile, and Exploration of the Nile Sources. Fifth Edition. Maps and Illustrations. Crown 8vo. 6*s.*

"*Charmingly written;*" *says the* SPECTATOR, "*full, as might be expected, of incident, and free from that wearisome reiteration of useless facts which is the drawback to almost all books of African travel.*"

THE NILE TRIBUTARIES OF ABYSSINIA, and the Sword Hunters of the Hamran Arabs. With Maps and Illustrations. Sixth Edition. Crown 8vo. 6*s.*

The TIMES *says:* "*It adds much to our information respecting Egyptian Abyssinia and the different races that spread over it. It contains, moreover, some notable instances of English daring and enterprising skill; it abounds in animated tales of exploits dear to the heart of the British sportsman; and it will attract even the least studious reader, as the author tells a story well, and can describe nature with uncommon power.*"

Bancroft.—THE HISTORY OF THE UNITED STATES OF AMERICA, FROM THE DISCOVERY OF THE CONTINENT. By GEORGE BANCROFT. New and thoroughly Revised Edition. Six Vols. Crown 8vo. 54*s.*

Barker (Lady).—Works by LADY BARKER:—

A YEAR'S HOUSEKEEPING IN SOUTH AFRICA. With Illustrations. New and Cheaper Edition. Crown 8vo. 6*s.*

"*We have to thank Lady Barker for a very amusing book, over which we have spent many a delightful hour, and of which we will not take leave without alluding to the ineffably droll illustrations which add so very much to the enjoyment of her clear and sparkling descriptions.*"—MORNING POST.

Beesly.—STORIES FROM THE HISTORY OF ROME. By Mrs. BEESLY. Extra fcap. 8vo. 2*s.* 6*d.*

"*A little book for which every cultivated and intelligent mother will be grateful for.*"—EXAMINER.

Bismarck—IN THE FRANCO-GERMAN WAR. An Authorized Translation from the German of Dr. MORITZ BUSCH. Two Vols. Crown 8vo. 18*s.*

The TIMES says:—"*The publication of Bismarck's after-dinner talk, whether discreet or not, will be of priceless biographical value, and Englishmen, at least, will not be disposed to quarrel with Dr. Busch for giving a picture as true to life as Boswell's 'Johnson' of the foremost practical genius that Germany has produced since Frederick the Great.*"

Blackburne.—BIOGRAPHY OF THE RIGHT HON. FRANCIS BLACKBURNE, Late Lord Chancellor of Ireland. Chiefly in connexion with his Public and Political Career. By his Son, EDWARD BLACKBURNE, Q.C. With Portrait Engraved by JEENS. 8vo. 12*s.*

Blanford (W. T.)—GEOLOGY AND ZOOLOGY OF ABYSSINIA. By W. T. BLANFORD. 8vo. 21*s.*

Brontë.—CHARLOTTE BRONTË. A Monograph. By T. WEMYSS REID. With Illustrations. Third Edition. Crown 8vo. 6*s.*

Mr. Reid's little volume, which is based largely on letters, hitherto unpublished, from Charlotte Brontë to her school-fellow and life-long friend, Miss Ellen Nussey, is meant to be a companion, and not a rival, to Mrs. Gaskell's well-known "Life." To speak of the advantage of making biography autobiographical by the liberal use of correspondence has she was by nature (as Mr. Reid puts it) "a happy and high-spirited girl, and that even to the very last she had the faculty of overcoming her sorrows by means of that steadfast courage which was her most precious possession, and to which she was indebted for her successive victories over trials and disappointments of no ordinary character."

The book is illustrated by a Portrait of the Rev. Patrick Brontë, several Views of Haworth and its neighbourhood, and a facsimile of one of the most characteristic of Charlotte's letters.

Brooke.—THE RAJA OF SARAWAK: an Account of Sir James Brooke, K.C.B., LL.D. Given chiefly through Letters or Journals. By GERTRUDE L. JACOB. With Portrait and Maps. Two Vols. 8vo. 25*s*.

"*They who read Miss Jacob's book—and all should read it: all who are under the delusion that in our time there is no scope for heroism, and no place for romantic adventure, and no place for enterprise and ambition—will see how incident is crowded upon incident, and struggle upon struggle, till in the very abundance of materials that come to her hand the authoress can scarcely stop to give sufficient distinctness to her wonderful narrative.*"—ACADEMY.

Brooke.—RECOLLECTIONS OF THE IRISH CHURCH. By RICHARD S. BROOKE, D.D., late Rector of Wyton, Hunts. Crown 8vo. 4*s*. 6*d*.

Bryce.—Works by JAMES BRYCE, D.C.L., Regius Professor of Civil Law, Oxford:—

THE HOLY ROMAN EMPIRE. Sixth Edition, Revised and Enlarged. Crown 8vo. 7*s*. 6*d*.

"*It exactly supplies a want: it affords a key to much which men read of in their books as isolated facts, but of which they have hitherto had no connected exposition set before them.*"—SATURDAY REVIEW.

TRANSCAUCASIA AND ARARAT: being Notes of a Vacation Tour in the Autumn of 1876. With an Illustration and Map. Third Edition. Crown 8vo. 9*s*.

"*Mr. Bryce has written a lively and at the same time an instructive description of the tour he made last year in and about the Caucasus. When well-informed a jurist travels into regions seldom visited, and even walks up a mountain so rarely scaled as Ararat, he is justified in thinking that the impressions he brings home are worthy of being communicated to the world at large, especially when a terrible war is casting a lurid glow over the countries he has lately surveyed.*"—ATHENÆUM.

Burgoyne.—POLITICAL AND MILITARY EPISODES DURING THE FIRST HALF OF THE REIGN OF GEORGE III. Derived from the Life and Correspondence of the Right Hon. J. Burgoyne, Lieut.-General in his Majesty's Army, and M.P. for Preston. By E. B. DE FONBLANQUE. With Portrait, Heliotype Plate, and Maps. 8vo. 16*s*.

Burke.—EDMUND BURKE, a Historical Study. By JOHN MORLEY, B.A., Oxon. Crown 8vo. 7*s*. 6*d*.

"*The style is terse and incisive, and brilliant with epigram and point. Its sustained power of reasoning, its wide sweep of observation and reflection, its elevated ethical and social tone, stamp it as a work of high excellence.*"—SATURDAY REVIEW.

Burrows.—WORTHIES OF ALL SOULS: Four Centuries of English History. Illustrated from the College Archives. By MONTAGU BURROWS, Chichele Professor of Modern History at Oxford, Fellow of All Souls. 8vo. 14*s.*

"*A most amusing as well as a most instructive book.*—GUARDIAN.

Campbell.—LOG-LETTERS FROM THE "CHALLENGER." By LORD GEORGE CAMPBELL. With Map. Fifth and cheaper Edition. Crown 8vo. 6*s.*

"*A delightful book, which we heartily commend to the general reader.*" —SATURDAY REVIEW.

"*We do not hesitate to say that anything so fresh, so picturesque, so generally delightful, as these log-letters has not appeared among books of travel for a long time.*"—EXAMINER.

"*A more lively and amusing record of travel we have not had the fortune to read for some time. The whole book is pervaded by a spirit of life, animation, and fun.*"—STANDARD.

Campbell.—MY CIRCULAR NOTES: Extracts from Journals; Letters sent Home; Geological and other Notes, written while Travelling Westwards round the World, from July 6th, 1874, to July 6th, 1875. By J. F. CAMPBELL, Author of "Frost and Fire." Cheaper Issue. Crown 8vo. 6*s.*

"*We have read numbers of books of travel, but we can call to mind few that have given us more genuine pleasure than this. A more agreeable style of narrative than his it is hardly possible to conceive. We seem to be accompanying him in his trip round the world, so life-like is his description of the countries he visited.*"—LAND AND WATER.

Campbell.—TURKS AND GREEKS. Notes of a recent Excursion. By the Hon. DUDLEY CAMPBELL, M.A. With Coloured Map. Crown 8vo. 3*s.* 6*d.*

Carstares.—WILLIAM CARSTARES: a Character and Career of the Revolutionary Epoch (1649—1715). By ROBERT STORY, Minister of Rosneath. 8vo. 12*s.*

Chatterton: A BIOGRAPHICAL STUDY. By DANIEL WILSON, LL.D., Professor of History and English Literature in University College, Toronto. Crown 8vo. 6*s.* 6*d.*

Chatterton: A STORY OF THE YEAR 1770. By Professor MASSON, LL.D. Crown 8vo. 5*s.*

Clark.—MEMORIALS FROM JOURNALS AND LETTERS OF SAMUEL CLARK, M.A., formerly Principal of the National Society's Training College, Battersea. Edited with Introduction by his WIFE. With Portrait. Crown 8vo. 7*s.* 6*d.*

Combe.—THE LIFE OF GEORGE COMBE, Author of "The Constitution of Man." By CHARLES GIBBON. With Three Portraits engraved by JEENS. Two Vols. 8vo. 32*s.*

"*A graphic and interesting account of the long life and indefatigable labours of a very remarkable man.*"—SCOTSMAN.

Cooper.—ATHENÆ CANTABRIGIENSES. By CHARLES HENRY COOPER, F.S.A., and THOMPSON COOPER, F.S.A. Vol. I. 8vo., 1500—85, 18*s.*; Vol. II., 1586—1609, 18*s.*

Correggio.—ANTONIO ALLEGRI DA CORREGGIO. From the German of Dr. JULIUS MEYER, Director of the Royal Gallery, Berlin. Edited, with an Introduction, by Mrs. HEATON. Containing Twenty Woodbury-type Illustrations. Royal 8vo. Cloth elegant. 31*s.* 6*d.*

Cox (G. V.)—RECOLLECTIONS OF OXFORD. By G. V. COX, M.A., New College, late Esquire Bedel and Coroner in the University of Oxford. *Cheaper Edition.* Crown 8vo. 6*s.*

Cunynghame (Sir A. T.)—MY COMMAND IN SOUTH AFRICA, 1874—78. Comprising Experiences of Travel in the Colonies of South Africa and the Independent States. By Sir ARTHUR THURLOW CUNYNGHAME, G.C.B., then Lieutenant-Governor and Commander of the Forces in South Africa. Third Edition. 8vo. 12*s.* 6*d.*

The TIMES *says*:—"*It is a volume of great interest, ... full of incidents which vividly illustrate the condition of the Colonies and the character and habits of the natives. . . . . It contains valuable illustrations of Cape warfare, and at the present moment it cannot fail to command wide-spread attention.*"

"Daily News."—THE DAILY NEWS' CORRESPONDENCE of the War between Germany and France, 1870—1. Edited with Notes and Comments. New Edition. Complete in One Volume. With Maps and Plans. Crown 8vo. 6*s.*

THE DAILY NEWS' CORRESPONDENCE of the War between Russia and Turkey, to the fall of Kars. Including the letters of Mr. Archibald Forbes, Mr. J. E. McGahan, and other Special Correspondents in Europe and Asia. Second Edition, enlarged. Cheaper Edition. Crown 8vo. 6*s.*

FROM THE FALL OF KARS TO THE CONCLUSION OF PEACE. Cheaper Edition. Crown 8vo. 6*s.*

Davidson.—THE LIFE OF A SCOTTISH PROBATIONER; being a Memoir of Thomas Davidson, with his Poems and Letters. By JAMES BROWN, Minister of St. James's Street Church, Paisley. Second Edition, revised and enlarged, with Portrait. Crown 8vo. 7*s.* 6*d.*

Deas.—THE RIVER CLYDE. An Historical Description of the Rise and Progress of the Harbour of Glasgow, and of the Improvement of the River from Glasgow to Port Glasgow. By J. DEAS, M. Inst. C.E. 8vo. 10*s*. 6*d*.

Denison.—A HISTORY OF CAVALRY FROM THE EARLIEST TIMES. With Lessons for the Future. By Lieut.-Col. GEORGE DENISON, Commanding the Governor-General's Body Guard, Canada, Author of "Modern Cavalry." With Maps and Plans. 8vo. 18*s*.

Dilke.—GREATER BRITAIN. A Record of Travel in English-speaking Countries during 1866-7. (America, Australia, India.) By Sir CHARLES WENTWORTH DILKE, M.P. Sixth Edition. Crown 8vo. 6*s*.

"*Many of the subjects discussed in these pages,*" *says the* DAILY NEWS, "*are of the widest interest, and such as no man who cares for the future of his race and of the world can afford to treat with indifference.*"

Doyle.—HISTORY OF AMERICA. By J. A. DOYLE. With Maps. 18mo. 4*s*. 6*d*.

"*Mr. Doyle's style is clear and simple, his facts are accurately stated, and his book is meritoriously free from prejudice on questions where partisanship runs high amongst us.*"—SATURDAY REVIEW.

Drummond of Hawthornden: THE STORY OF HIS LIFE AND WRITINGS. By PROFESSOR MASSON. With Portrait and Vignette engraved by C. H. JEENS. Crown 8vo. 10*s*. 6*d*.

Duff.—Works by M. E. GRANT-DUFF, M.P., late Under Secretary of State for India:—

NOTES OF AN INDIAN JOURNEY. With Map. 8vo. 10*s*. 6*d*.

"*These notes are full of pleasant remarks and illustrations, borrowed from every kind of source.*"—SATURDAY REVIEW.

MISCELLANIES POLITICAL AND LITERARY. 8vo. 10*s*. 6*d*.

Eadie.—LIFE OF JOHN EADIE, D.D., LL.D. By JAMES BROWN, D.D., Author of "The Life of a Scottish Probationer." With Portrait. Second Edition. Crown 8vo. 7*s*. 6*d*.

"*An ably written and characteristic biography.*"—TIMES.

Elliott.—LIFE OF HENRY VENN ELLIOTT, of Brighton. By JOSIAH BATEMAN, M.A. With Portrait, engraved by JEENS. Extra fcap. 8vo. Third and Cheaper Edition. 6*s*.

Elze.—ESSAYS ON SHAKESPEARE. By Dr. KARL ELZE. Translated with the Author's sanction by L. DORA SCHMITZ. 8vo. 12*s*.

"*A more desirable contribution to criticism has not recently been made.*" —ATHENÆUM.

English Men of Letters. Edited by JOHN MORLEY. A Series of Short Books to tell people what is best worth knowing as to the Life, Character, and Works of some of the great English Writers. In crown 8vo. Price 2*s.* 6*d.* each.

I. DR. JOHNSON. By LESLIE STEPHEN.

"*The new series opens well with Mr. Leslie Stephen's sketch of Dr. Johnson. It could hardly have been done better; and it will convey to the readers for whom it is intended a juster estimate of Johnson than either of the two essays of Lord Macaulay.*"—PALL MALL GAZETTE.

II. SIR WALTER SCOTT. By R. H. HUTTON.

"*The tone of the volume is excellent throughout.*"—ATHENÆUM.

"*We could not wish for a more suggestive introduction to Scott and his poems and novels.*"—EXAMINER.

III. GIBBON. By J. C. MORISON.

"*As a clear, thoughtful, and attractive record of the life and works of the greatest among the world's historians, it deserves the highest praise.*"—EXAMINER.

IV. SHELLEY. By J. A. SYMONDS.

"*The lovers of this great poet are to be congratulated on having at their command so fresh, clear, and intelligent a presentment of the subject, written by a man of adequate and wide culture.*"—ATHENÆUM.

V. HUME. By Professor HUXLEY.

"*It may fairly be said that no one now living could have expounded Hume with more sympathy or with equal perspicuity.*"—ATHENÆUM.

VI. GOLDSMITH. By WILLIAM BLACK.

"*Mr. Black brings a fine sympathy and taste to bear in his criticism of Goldsmith's writings as well as in his sketch of the incidents of his life.*" ATHENÆUM.

VII. DEFOE. By W. MINTO.

"*Mr. Minto's book is careful and accurate in all that is stated, and faithful in all that it suggests. It will repay reading more than once.*" -ATHENÆUM.

VIII. BURNS. By Principal SHAIRP, Professor of Poetry in the University of Oxford.

"*It is impossible to desire fairer criticism than Principal Shairp's on Burns's poetry . . . . . None of the series has given a truer estimate either of character or of genius than this little volume . . . . . and all who read it will be thoroughly grateful to the author for this monument to the genius of Scotland's greatest poet.*"—SPECTATOR.

IX. SPENSER. By the Very Rev. the DEAN OF ST. PAUL'S.

"*Dr. Church is master of his subject, and writes always with good taste.*"—ACADEMY.

X. THACKERAY. By ANTHONY TROLLOPE.

"*Mr. Trollope's sketch is excellently adapted to fufil the purpose of the series in which it appears.*"—ATHENÆUM.

English Men of Letters.—*continued.*

BURKE. By JOHN MORLEY.
MILTON. By MARK PATTISON. } [*Nearly ready.*

Others in preparation.

Eton College, History of. By H. C. MAXWELL LYTE, M.A. With numerous Illustrations by Professor DELAMOTTE, Coloured Plates, and a Steel Portrait of the Founder, engraved by C. H. JEENS. New and cheaper Issue, with Corrections. Medium 8vo. Cloth elegant. 21*s.*

"*Hitherto no account of the College, with all its associations, has appeared which can compare either in completeness or in interest with this. . . . It is indeed a book worthy of the ancient renown of King Henry's College.*"—DAILY NEWS.

"*We are at length presented with a work on England's greatest public school, worthy of the subject of which it treats. . . . A really valuable and authentic history of Eton College.*"—GUARDIAN.

European History, Narrated in a Series of Historical Selections from the best Authorities. Edited and arranged by E. M. SEWELL and C. M. YONGE. First Series, crown 8vo. 6*s.*; Second Series, 1088–1228, crown 8vo. 6*s.* Third Edition.

"*We know of scarcely anything,*" *says the* GUARDIAN, *of this volume,* "*which is so likely to raise to a higher level the average standard of English education.*"

Faraday.—MICHAEL FARADAY. By J. H. GLADSTONE, Ph.D., F.R.S. Second Edition, with Portrait engraved by JEENS from a photograph by J. WATKINS. Crown 8vo. 4*s.* 6*d.*

PORTRAIT. Artist's Proof. 5*s.*

Forbes.—LIFE AND LETTERS OF JAMES DAVID FORBES, F.R.S., late Principal of the United College in the University of St. Andrews. By J. C. SHAIRP, LL.D., Principal of the United College in the University of St. Andrews; P. G. TAIT, M.A., Professor of Natural Philosophy in the University of Edinburgh; and A. ADAMS-REILLY, F.R.G.S. 8vo. with Portraits, Map, and Illustrations, 16*s.*

Freeman.—Works by EDWARD A. FREEMAN, D.C.L., LL.D.:—

HISTORICAL ESSAYS. Third Edition. 8vo. 10*s.* 6*d.*

CONTENTS:—*I.* "*The Mythical and Romantic Elements in Early English History;*" *II.* "*The Continuity of English History;*" *III.* "*The Relations between the Crowns of England and Scotland;*" *IV.* "*St. Thomas of Canterbury and his Biographers;*" *V.* "*The Reign of Edward the Third:*" *VI.* "*The Holy Roman Empire;*" *VII.* "*The Franks and the Gauls;*" *VIII.* "*The Early Sieges of Paris;*" *IX.* "*Frederick the First, King of Italy;*" *X.* "*The Emperor Frederick the Second;*" *XI.* "*Charles the Bold;*" *XII.* "*Presidential Government.*

Freeman—*continued.*

A SECOND SERIES OF HISTORICAL ESSAYS. 8vo. 10*s.* 6*d.*

The principal Essays are:—"Ancient Greece and Mediæval Italy:" "Mr. Gladstone's Homer and the Homeric Ages:" "The Historians of Athens:" "The Athenian Democracy:" "Alexander the Great:" "Greece during the Macedonian Period:" "Mommsen's History of Rome:" "Lucius Cornelius Sulla:" "The Flavian Cæsars."

HISTORICAL ESSAYS. Third Series. [*In the press.*

COMPARATIVE POLITICS.—Lectures at the Royal Institution. To which is added the "Unity of History," the Rede Lecture at Cambridge, 1872. 8vo. 14*s.*

THE HISTORY AND CONQUESTS OF THE SARACENS. Six Lectures. Third Edition, with New Preface. Crown 8vo. 3*s.* 6*d.*

HISTORICAL AND ARCHITECTURAL SKETCHES: chiefly Italian. With Illustrations by the Author. Crown 8vo. 10*s.* 6*d.*

"*Mr. Freeman may here be said to give us a series of 'notes on the spot' in illustration of the intimate relations of History and Architecture, and this is done in so masterly a manner—there is so much freshness, so much knowledge so admirably condensed, that we are almost tempted to say that we prefer these sketches to his more elaborate studies.*"—NONCONFORMIST.

HISTORY OF FEDERAL GOVERNMENT, from the Foundation of the Achaian League to the Disruption of the United States. Vol. I. General Introduction. History of the Greek Federations. 8vo. 21*s.*

OLD ENGLISH HISTORY. With *Five Coloured Maps.* Fourth Edition. Extra fcap. 8vo., half-bound. 6*s.*

"*The book indeed is full of instruction and interest to students of all ages, and he must be a well-informed man indeed who will not rise from its perusal with clearer and more accurate ideas of a too much neglected portion of English history.*"—SPECTATOR.

HISTORY OF THE CATHEDRAL CHURCH OF WELLS, as illustrating the History of the Cathedral Churches of the Old Foundation. Crown 8vo. 3*s.* 6*d.*

"*The history assumes in Mr. Freeman's hands a significance, and, we may add, a practical value as suggestive of what a cathedral ought to be, which make it well worthy of mention.*"—SPECTATOR.

THE GROWTH OF THE ENGLISH CONSTITUTION FROM THE EARLIEST TIMES. Crown 8vo. 5*s.* Third Edition, revised.

Freeman—*continued.*

GENERAL SKETCH OF EUROPEAN HISTORY. Being Vol. I. of a Historical Course for Schools edited by E. A. FREEMAN. New Edition, enlarged with Maps, Chronological Table, Index, &c. 18mo. 3*s.* 6*d.*

"*It supplies the great want of a good foundation for historical teaching. The scheme is an excellent one, and this instalment has been accepted in a way that promises much for the volumes that are yet to appear.*"—EDUCATIONAL TIMES.

THE OTTOMAN POWER IN EUROPE: its Nature, its Growth, and its Decline. With Three Coloured Maps. Crown 8vo. 7*s.* 6*d.*

Galileo.—THE PRIVATE LIFE OF GALILEO. Compiled principally from his Correspondence and that of his eldest daughter, Sister Maria Celeste, Nun in the Franciscan Convent of S. Matthew in Arcetri. With Portrait. Crown 8vo. 7*s.* 6*d.*

Geddes.—THE PROBLEM OF THE HOMERIC POEMS. By W. D. GEDDES, LL.D., Professor of Greek in the University of Aberdeen. 8vo. 14*s.*

Gladstone—Works by the Right Hon. W. E. GLADSTONE, M.P.:—

JUVENTUS MUNDI. The Gods and Men of the Heroic Age. Crown 8vo. cloth. With Map. 10*s.* 6*d.* Second Edition.

"*Seldom,*" *says the* ATHENÆUM, "*out of the great poems themselves, have these Divinities looked so majestic and respectable. To read these brilliant details is like standing on the Olympian threshold and gazing at the ineffable brightness within.*"

HOMERIC SYNCHRONISM. An inquiry into the Time and Place of Homer. Crown 8vo. 6*s.*

"*It is impossible not to admire the immense range of thought and inquiry which the author has displayed.*"—BRITISH QUARTERLY REVIEW.

Goethe and Mendelssohn (1821—1831). Translated from the German of Dr. KARL MENDELSSOHN, Son of the Composer, by M. E. VON GLEHN. From the Private Diaries and Home Letters of Mendelssohn, with Poems and Letters of Goethe never before printed. Also with two New and Original Portraits, Facsimiles, and Appendix of Twenty Letters hitherto unpublished. Crown 8vo. 5*s.* Second Edition, enlarged.

" . . . *Every page is full of interest, not merely to the musician, but to the general reader. The book is a very charming one, on a topic of deep and lasting interest.*"—STANDARD.

Goldsmid.—TELEGRAPH AND TRAVEL. A Narrative of the Formation and Development of Telegraphic Communication between England and India, under the orders of Her Majesty's Government, with incidental Notices of the Countries traversed by the Lines. By Colonel Sir FREDERIC GOLDSMID, C.B., K.C.S.I., late Director of the Government Indo-European Telegraph. With numerous Illustrations and Maps. 8vo. 21*s.*

"*The merit of the work is a total absence of exaggeration, which does not, however, preclude a vividness and vigour of style not always characteristic of similar narratives.*"—STANDARD.

Gordon.—LAST LETTERS FROM EGYPT, to which are added Letters from the Cape. By LADY DUFF GORDON. With a Memoir by her Daughter, Mrs. Ross, and Portrait engraved by JEENS. Second Edition. Crown 8vo. 9*s.*

"*The intending tourist who wishes to acquaint himself with the country he is about to visit, stands embarrassed amidst the riches presented for his choice, and in the end probably rests contented with the sober usefulness of Murray. He will not, however, if he is well advised, grudge a place in his portmanteau to this book.*"—TIMES.

Gray.—CHINA. A History of the Laws, Manners, and Customs of the People. By the VENERABLE JOHN HENRY GRAY. LL.D., Archdeacon of Hong Kong, formerly H.B.M. Consular Chaplain at Canton. Edited by W. Gow Gregor. With 150 Full-page Illustrations, being Facsimiles of Drawings by a Chinese Artist. 2 Vols. Demy 8vo. 32*s.*

"*Its pages contain the most truthful and vivid picture of Chinese life which has ever been published.*"—ATHENÆUM.

"*The only elaborate and valuable book we have had for many years treating generally of the people of the Celestial Empire.*"—ACADEMY.

Green.—Works by JOHN RICHARD GREEN:—

HISTORY OF THE ENGLISH PEOPLE. Vol. I.—Early England—Foreign Kings—The Charter—The Parliament. With 8 Coloured Maps. 8vo. 16*s.* Vol. II.—The Monarchy, 1461—1540; the Restoration, 1540—1603. 8vo. 16*s.* Vol. III.—Puritan England, 1603—1660; the Revolution, 1660—1688. With 4 Maps. 8vo. 16*s.* [*Vol. IV. in the press.*

"*Mr. Green has done a work which probably no one but himself could have done. He has read and assimilated the results of all the labours of students during the last half century in the field of English history, and has given them a fresh meaning by his own independent study. He has fused together by the force of sympathetic imagination all that he has so collected, and has given us a vivid and forcible sketch of the march of English history. His book, both in its aims and its accomplishments, rises far beyond any of a similar kind, and it will give the colouring to the popular view to English history for some time to come.*"—EXAMINER.

Green.—*continued.*

A SHORT HISTORY OF THE ENGLISH PEOPLE. With Coloured Maps, Genealogical Tables, and Chronological Annals. Crown 8vo. 8*s.* 6*d.* Sixty-first Thousand.

"*To say that Mr. Green's book is better than those which have preceded it, would be to convey a very inadequate impression of its merits. It stands alone as the one general history of the country, for the sake of which all others, if young and old are wise, will be speedily and surely set aside.*"

STRAY STUDIES FROM ENGLAND AND ITALY. Crown 8vo. 8*s.* 6*d.* Containing: Lambeth and the Archbishops—The Florence of Dante—Venice and Rome—Early History of Oxford—The District Visitor—Capri—Hotels in the Clouds—Sketches in Sunshine, &c.

"*One and all of the papers are eminently readable.*"—ATHENÆUM.

Guest.—LECTURES ON THE HISTORY OF ENGLAND. By M. J. GUEST. With Maps. Crown 8vo. 6*s.*

Hamerton.—Works by P. G. HAMERTON:—

THE INTELLECTUAL LIFE. With a Portrait of Leonardo da Vinci, etched by LEOPOLD FLAMENG. Second Edition. Crown 8vo. 10*s.* 6*d.*

"*We have read the whole book with great pleasure, and we can recommend it strongly to all who can appreciate grave reflections on a very important subject, excellently illustrated from the resources of a mind stored with much reading and much keen observation of real life.*"—SATURDAY REVIEW.

THOUGHTS ABOUT ART. New Edition, revised, with an Introduction. Crown 8vo. 8*s.* 6*d.*

"*A manual of sound and thorough criticism on art.*"—STANDARD.

Hill.—THE RECORDER OF BIRMINGHAM. A Memoir of Matthew Davenport Hill, with Selections from his Correspondence. By his Daughters ROSAMOND and FLORENCE DAVENPORT-HILL. With Portrait engraved by C. H. JEENS. 8vo. 16*s.*

Hill.—WHAT WE SAW IN AUSTRALIA. By ROSAMOND and FLORENCE HILL. Crown 8vo. 10*s.* 6*d.*

"*May be recommended as an interesting and truthful picture of the condition of those lands which are so distant and yet so much like home.*"—SATURDAY REVIEW.

Hodgson.—MEMOIR OF REV. FRANCIS HODGSON, B.D., Scholar, Poet, and Divine. By his Son, the Rev. JAMES T. HODGSON, M.A. Containing numerous Letters from Lord Byron and others. With Portrait engraved by JEENS. Two Vols. Crown 8vo. 18*s*.

"*A book that has added so much of a healthy nature to our knowledge of Byron, and that contains so rich a store of delightful correspondence.*" —ATHENÆUM.

Hole.—A GENEALOGICAL STEMMA OF THE KINGS OF ENGLAND AND FRANCE. By the Rev. C. HOLE, M.A., Trinity College, Cambridge. On Sheet, 1*s*.

A BRIEF BIOGRAPHICAL DICTIONARY. Compiled and Arranged by the Rev. CHARLES HOLE, M.A. Second Edition. 18mo. 4*s*. 6*d*.

Hooker and Ball.—MAROCCO AND THE GREAT ATLAS: Journal of a Tour in. By Sir JOSEPH D. HOOKER, K.C.S.I., C.B., F.R.S., &c., and JOHN BALL, F.R.S. With an Appendix, including a Sketch of the Geology of Marocco, by G. MAW, F.L.S., F.G.S. With Illustrations and Map. 8vo. 21*s*.

Hozier (H. M.)—Works by CAPTAIN HENRY M. HOZIER, late Assistant Military Secretary to Lord Napier of Magdala:—

THE SEVEN WEEKS' WAR; Its Antecedents and Incidents. *New and Cheaper Edition.* With New Preface, Maps, and Plans. Crown 8vo. 6*s*.

"*All that Mr. Hozier saw of the great events of the war—and he saw a large share of them—he describes in clear and vivid language.*"—SATURDAY REVIEW.

THE INVASIONS OF ENGLAND: a History of the Past, with Lessons for the Future. Two Vols. 8vo. 28*s*.

The PALL MALL GAZETTE says:—"*As to all invasions executed, or deliberately projected but not carried out, from the landing of Julius Cæsar to the raising of the Boulogne camp, Captain Hozier furnishes copious and most interesting particulars.*"

Hübner.—A RAMBLE ROUND THE WORLD IN 1871. By M. LE BARON HÜBNER, formerly Ambassador and Minister. Translated by LADY HERBERT. New and Cheaper Edition. With numerous Illustrations. Crown 8vo. 6*s*.

"*It is difficult to do ample justice to this pleasant narrative of travel . . . . it does not contain a single dull paragraph.*"—MORNING POST.

Hughes.—Works by THOMAS HUGHES, Q.C., Author of "Tom Brown's School Days."

ALFRED THE GREAT. New Edition. Crown 8vo. 6*s*.

Hughes.—*continued.*

MEMOIR OF A BROTHER. With Portrait of GEORGE HUGHES, after WATTS. Engraved by JEENS. Crown 8vo. 5*s.* Sixth Edition.

"*The boy who can read this book without deriving from it some additional impulse towards honourable, manly, and independent conduct, has no good stuff in him.*"—DAILY NEWS.

Hunt.—HISTORY OF ITALY. By the Rev. W. HUNT, M.A. Being the Fourth Volume of the Historical Course for Schools. Edited by EDWARD A. FREEMAN, D.C.L. 18mo. 3*s.*

"*Mr. Hunt gives us a most compact but very readable little book, containing in small compass a very complete outline of a complicated and perplexing subject. It is a book which may be safely recommended to others besides schoolboys.*"—JOHN BULL.

Irving.—THE ANNALS OF OUR TIME. A Diurnal of Events, Social and Political, Home and Foreign, from the Accession of Queen Victoria to the Peace of Versailles. By JOSEPH IRVING. *Fourth Edition.* 8vo. half-bound. 16*s.*

ANNALS OF OUR TIME. Supplement. From Feb. 28, 1871, to March 19, 1874. 8vo. 4*s.* 6*d.*

ANNALS OF OUR TIME. Second Supplement. From March, 1874, to the Occupation of Cyprus. 8vo. 4*s.* 6*d.*

"*We have before us a trusty and ready guide to the events of the past thirty years, available equally for the statesman, the politician, the public writer, and the general reader.*"—TIMES.

James.—Works by HENRY JAMES, Jun. FRENCH POETS AND NOVELISTS. Crown 8vo. 8*s.* 6*d.*

CONTENTS:—*Alfred de Musset; Théophile Gautier; Baudelaire; Honoré de Balzac; George Sand; The Two Ampères; Turgenieff, &c.*

Johnson's Lives of the Poets.—The Six Chief Lives—Milton, Dryden, Swift, Addison, Pope, Gray. With Macaulay's "Life of Johnson." Edited, with Preface, by MATTHEW ARNOLD. Crown 8vo. 6*s.*

Killen.—ECCLESIASTICAL HISTORY OF IRELAND, from the Earliest Date to the Present Time. By W. D. KILLEN, D.D., President of Assembly's College, Belfast, and Professor of Ecclesiastical History. Two Vols. 8vo. 25*s.*

"*Those who have the leisure will do well to read these two volumes. They are full of interest, and are the result of great research. . . . We have no hesitation in recommending the work to all who wish to improve their acquaintance with Irish history.*"—SPECTATOR.

Kingsley (Charles).—Works by the Rev. CHARLES KINGSLEY, M.A., Rector of Eversley and Canon of Westminster. (For other Works by the same Author, *see* THEOLOGICAL and BELLES LETTRES Catalogues.)

ON THE ANCIEN RÉGIME as it existed on the Continent before the FRENCH REVOLUTION. Three Lectures delivered at the Royal Institution. Crown 8vo. 6*s.*

AT LAST: A CHRISTMAS in the WEST INDIES. With nearly Fifty Illustrations. Fifth Edition. Crown 8vo. 6*s.*

Mr. Kingsley's dream of forty years was at last fulfilled, when he started on a Christmas expedition to the West Indies, for the purpose of becoming personally acquainted with the scenes which he has so vividly described in "Westward Ho!" These two volumes are the journal of his voyage. Records of natural history, sketches of tropical landscape, chapters on education, views of society, all find their place. "We can only say that Mr. Kingsley's account of a 'Christmas in the West Indies' is in every way worthy to be classed among his happiest productions."—STANDARD.

THE ROMAN AND THE TEUTON. A Series of Lectures delivered before the University of Cambridge. New and Cheaper Edition, with Preface by Professor MAX MÜLLER. Crown 8vo. 6*s.*

PLAYS AND PURITANS, and other Historical Essays. With Portrait of Sir WALTER RALEIGH. New Edition. Crown 8vo. 6*s.*

In addition to the Essay mentioned in the title, this volume contains other two—one on "Sir Walter Raleigh and his Time," and one on Froude's "History of England."

Kingsley (Henry).—TALES OF OLD TRAVEL. Re-narrated by HENRY KINGSLEY, F.R.G.S. With *Eight Illustrations* by HUARD. Fifth Edition. Crown 8vo. 5*s.*

"We know no better book for those who want knowledge or seek to refresh it. As for the 'sensational,' most novels are tame compared with these narratives."—ATHENÆUM.

Lang.—CYPRUS: Its History, its Present Resources and Future Prospects. By R. HAMILTON LANG, late H.M. Consul for the Island of Cyprus. With Two Illustrations and Four Maps. 8vo. 14*s.*

"The fair and impartial account of her past and present to be found in these pages has an undoubted claim on the attention of all intelligent readers."—MORNING POST.

Laocoon.—Translated from the Text of Lessing, with Preface and Notes by the Right Hon. SIR ROBERT J. PHILLIMORE, D.C.L. With Photographs. 8vo. 12*s.*

Leonardo da Vinci and his Works.—Consisting of a Life of Leonardo Da Vinci, by MRS. CHARLES W. HEATON, Author of "Albrecht Dürer of Nürnberg," &c., an Essay on his Scientific and Literary Works by CHARLES CHRISTOPHER BLACK, M.A., and an account of his more important Paintings and Drawings. Illustrated with Permanent Photographs. Royal 8vo, cloth, extra gilt. 31*s.* 6*d.*

"*A beautiful volume, both without and within. Messrs. Macmillan are conspicuous among publishers for the choice binding and printing of their books, and this is got up in their best style. . . . No English publication that we know of has so thoroughly and attractively collected together all that is known of Leonardo.*"—TIMES.

Liechtenstein.—HOLLAND HOUSE. By Princess MARIE LIECHTENSTEIN. With Five Steel Engravings by C. H. JEENS, after Paintings by WATTS and other celebrated Artists, and numerous Illustrations drawn by Professor P. H. DELAMOTTE, and engraved on Wood by J. D. COOPER, W. PALMER, and JEWITT & Co. Third and Cheaper Edition. Medium 8vo. cloth elegant. 16*s.*

Also, an Edition containing, in addition to the above, about 40 Illustrations by the Woodbury-type process, and India Proofs of the Steel Engravings. Two vols. medium 4to. half morocco elegant. 4*l.* 4*s.*

"*When every strictly just exception shall have been taken, she may be conscientiously congratulated by the most scrupulous critic on the production of a useful, agreeable, beautifully-illustrated, and attractive book.*"—TIMES. "*It would take up more room than we can spare to enumerate all the interesting suggestions and notes which are to be found in these volumes. . . . . The woodcuts are admirable, and some of the autographs are very interesting.*"—PALL MALL GAZETTE.

Lloyd.—THE AGE OF PERICLES. A History of the Arts and Politics of Greece from the Persian to the Peloponnesian War. By W. WATKISS LLOYD. Two Vols. 8vo. 21*s.*

"*No such account of Greek art of the best period has yet been brought together in an English work. . . . . Mr. Lloyd has produced a book of unusual excellence and interest.*"—PALL MALL GAZETTE.

Macarthur.—HISTORY OF SCOTLAND, By MARGARET MACARTHUR. Being the Third Volume of the Historical Course for Schools, Edited by EDWARD A. FREEMAN, D.C.L. Second Edition. 18mo. 2*s.*

"*It is an excellent summary, unimpeachable as to facts, and putting them in the clearest and most impartial light attainable.*"—GUARDIAN. "*No previous History of Scotland of the same bulk is anything like so trustworthy, or deserves to be so extensively used as a text-book.*"—GLOBE.

Macmillan (Rev. Hugh).—For other Works by same Author, *see* THEOLOGICAL and SCIENTIFIC CATALOGUES.

HOLIDAYS ON HIGH LANDS; or, Rambles and Incidents in search of Alpine Plants. Second Edition, revised and enlarged. Globe 8vo. cloth. 6*s*.

"*Botanical knowledge is blended with a love of nature, a pious enthusiasm, and a rich felicity of diction not to be met with in any works of kindred character, if we except those of Hugh Miller.*"—TELEGRAPH.
"*Mr. Macmillan's glowing pictures of Scandinavian scenery.*"—SATURDAY REVIEW.

Macready.—MACREADY'S REMINISCENCES AND SELECTIONS FROM HIS DIARIES AND LETTERS. Edited by Sir F. POLLOCK, Bart., one of his Executors. With Four Portraits engraved by JEENS. New and Cheaper Edition. Crown 8vo. 7*s*. 6*d*.

"*As a careful and for the most part just estimate of the stage during a very brilliant period, the attraction of these volumes can scarcely be surpassed. . . . Readers who have no special interest in theatrical matters, but enjoy miscellaneous gossip, will be allured from page to page, attracted by familiar names and by observations upon popular actors and authors.*"—SPECTATOR.

Mahaffy.—Works by the Rev. J. P. MAHAFFY, M.A., Fellow of Trinity College, Dublin:—

SOCIAL LIFE IN GREECE FROM HOMER TO MENANDER. Third Edition, revised and enlarged, with a new chapter on Greek Art. Crown 8vo. 9*s*.

"*It should be in the hands of all who desire thoroughly to understand and to enjoy Greek literature, and to get an intelligent idea of the old Greek life, political, social, and religious.*"—GUARDIAN.

RAMBLES AND STUDIES IN GREECE. With Illustrations. Crown 8vo. 10*s*. 6*d*. New and enlarged Edition, with Map and Illustrations

"*A singularly instructive and agreeable volume.*"—ATHENÆUM.

"Maori."—SPORT AND WORK ON THE NEPAUL FRONTIER; or, Twelve Years' Sporting Reminiscences of an Indigo Planter. By "MAORI." With Illustrations. 8vo. 14*s*.

Margary.—THE JOURNEY OF AUGUSTUS RAYMOND MARGARY FROM SHANGHAE TO BHAMO AND BACK TO MANWYNE. From his Journals and Letters, with a brief Biographical Preface, a concluding chapter by Sir RUTHERFORD ALCOCK, K.C.B., and a Steel Portrait engraved by JEENS, and Map. 8vo. 10*s*. 6*d*.

"*There is a manliness, a cheerful spirit, an inherent vigour which was never overcome by sickness or debility, a tact which conquered the prejudices of a strange and suspicious population, a quiet self-reliance, always combined with deep religious feeling, unalloyed by either priggishness, cant, or superstition, that ought to commend this volume to readers sitting quietly at home who feel any pride in the high estimation accorded to men of their race at Yarkand or at Khiva, in the heart of Africa, or on the shores of Lake Seri-kul."*—SATURDAY REVIEW.

Markham.—NORTHWARD HO! By Captain ALBERT H. MARKHAM, R.N., Author of "The Great Frozen Sea," &c. Including a Narrative of Captain Phipps's Expedition, by a Midshipman. With Illustrations. Crown 8vo. 10*s.* 6*d.*

Martin.—THE HISTORY OF LLOYD'S, AND OF MARINE INSURANCE IN GREAT BRITAIN. With an Appendix containing Statistics relating to Marine Insurance. By FREDERICK MARTIN, Author of "The Statesman's Year Book." 8vo. 14*s.*

Martineau.—BIOGRAPHICAL SKETCHES, 1852—1875. By HARRIET MARTINEAU. With Additional Sketches, and Autobiographical Sketch. Fifth Edition. Crown 8vo. 6*s.*

"*Miss Martineau's large literary powers and her fine intellectual training make these little sketches more instructive, and constitute them more genuinely works of art, than many more ambitious and diffuse biographies."*—FORTNIGHTLY REVIEW.

Masson (David).—For other Works by same Author, *see* PHILOSOPHICAL and BELLES LETTRES CATALOGUES.

CHATTERTON: A Story of the Year 1770. By DAVID MASSON, LL.D., Professor of Rhetoric and English Literature in the University of Edinburgh. Crown 8vo. 5*s.*

THE THREE DEVILS: Luther's, Goethe's, and Milton's; and other Essays. Crown 8vo. 5*s.*

WORDSWORTH, SHELLEY, AND KEATS; and other Essays. Crown 8vo. 5*s.*

Mathews.—LIFE OF CHARLES J. MATHEWS, Chiefly Autobiographical. With Selections from his Correspondence and Speeches. Edited by CHARLES DICKENS.

"*The book is a charming one from first to last, and Mr. Dickens deserves a full measure of credit for the care and discrimination he has exercised in the business of editing."*—GLOBE.

Maurice.—THE FRIENDSHIP OF BOOKS; AND OTHER LECTURES. By the REV. F. D. MAURICE. Edited with Preface, by THOMAS HUGHES, Q.C. Crown 8vo. 10*s.* 6*d.*

"*The high, pure, sympathetic, and truly charitable nature of Mr. Maurice is delightfully visible throughout these lectures, which are excellently adapted to spread a love of literature amongst the people."*—DAILY NEWS.

Mayor (J. E. B.)—WORKS edited by JOHN E. B. MAYOR, M.A., Kennedy Professor of Latin at Cambridge :—

CAMBRIDGE IN THE SEVENTEENTH CENTURY. Part II. Autobiography of Matthew Robinson. Fcap. 8vo. 5*s*. 6*d*.

LIFE OF BISHOP BEDELL. By his SON. Fcap. 8vo. 3*s*. 6*d*.

Melbourne.—MEMOIRS OF THE RT. HON. WILLIAM, SECOND VISCOUNT MELBOURNE. By W. M. TORRENS, M.P. With Portrait after Sir. T. Lawrence. Second Edition. 2 Vols. 8vo. 32*s*.

"*As might be expected, he has produced a book which will command and reward attention. It contains a great deal of valuable matter and a great deal of animated, elegant writing.*"—QUARTERLY REVIEW.

Mendelssohn.—LETTERS AND RECOLLECTIONS. By FERDINAND HILLER. Translated by M. E. VON GLEHN. With Portrait from a Drawing by KARL MÜLLER, never before published. Second Edition. Crown 8vo. 7*s*. 6*d*.

"*This is a very interesting addition to our knowledge of the great German composer. It reveals him to us under a new light, as the warm-hearted comrade, the musician whose soul was in his work, and the home-loving, domestic man.*"—STANDARD.

Merewether.—BY SEA AND BY LAND. Being a Trip through Egypt, India, Ceylon, Australia, New Zealand, and America—all Round the World. By HENRY ALWORTH MEREWETHER, one of Her Majesty's Counsel. Crown 8vo. 8*s*. 6*d*.

Michael Angelo Buonarotti; Sculptor, Painter, Architect. The Story of his Life and Labours. By C. C. BLACK, M.A. Illustrated by 20 Permanent Photographs. Royal 8vo. cloth elegant, 31*s*. 6*d*.

"*The story of Michael Angelo's life remains interesting whatever be the manner of telling it, and supported as it is by this beautiful series of photographs, the volume must take rank among the most splendid of Christmas books, fitted to serve and to outlive the season.*"—PALL MALL GAZETTE.

Michelet.—A SUMMARY OF MODERN HISTORY. Translated from the French of M. MICHELET, and continued to the present time by M. C. M. SIMPSON. Globe 8vo. 4*s*. 6*d*.

Milton.—LIFE OF JOHN MILTON. Narrated in connection with the Political, Ecclesiastical, and Literary History of his Time. By DAVID MASSON, M.A., LL.D., Professor of Rhetoric and English Literature in the University of Edinburgh. With Portraits. Vol. I. 18*s*. Vol. II., 1638—1643. 8vo. 16*s*. Vol. III. 1643—1649. 8vo. 18*s*. Vols. IV. and V. 1649—1660. 32*s*. Vol. VI. in the press.

This work is not only a Biography, but also a continuous Political, Ecclesiastical, and Literary History of England through Milton's whole time.

Mitford (A. B.)—TALES OF OLD JAPAN. By A. B. MITFORD, Second Secretary to the British Legation in Japan. With upwards of 30 Illustrations, drawn and cut on Wood by Japanese Artists. New and Cheaper Edition. Crown 8vo. 6*s.*

"*These very original volumes will always be interesting as memorials of a most exceptional society, while regarded simply as tales, they are sparkling, sensational, and dramatic, and the originality of their idea and the quaintness of their language give them a most captivating piquancy. The illustrations are extremely interesting, and for the curious in such matters have a special and particular value.*"—PALL MALL GAZETTE.

Monteiro.—ANGOLA AND THE RIVER CONGO. By JOACHIM MONTEIRO. With numerous Illustrations from Sketches taken on the spot, and a Map. Two Vols. crown 8vo. 21*s.*

"*Gives the first detailed account of a part of tropical Africa which is little known to Englishmen. . . . . The remarks on the geography and zoology of the country and the manners and customs of the various races inhabiting it, are extremely curious and interesting.*"—SATURDAY REVIEW. "*Full of valuable information and much picturesque description.*" PALL MALL GAZETTE.

Morison.—THE LIFE AND TIMES OF SAINT BERNARD, Abbot of Clairvaux. By JAMES COTTER MORISON, M.A. New Edition. Crown 8vo. 6*s.*

Moseley.—NOTES BY A NATURALIST ON THE *CHALLENGER*: being an Account of various Observations made during the Voyage of H.M.S. *Challenger*, Round the World, in 1872–76. By H. N. MOSELEY, F.R.S., Member of the Scientific Staff of the *Challenger*. 8vo. with Maps, Coloured Plates, and Woodcuts. 21*s.*

Murray.—ROUND ABOUT FRANCE. By E. C. GRENVILLE MURRAY. Crown 8vo. 7*s.* 6*d.*

"*These short essays are a perfect mine of information as to the present condition and future prospects of political parties in France. . . . It is at once extremely interesting and exceptionally instructive on a subject on which few English people are well informed.*"—SCOTSMAN.

Napier.—MACVEY NAPIER'S SELECTED CORRESPONDENCE. Edited by his Son, MACVEY NAPIER. 8vo, 14*s.*

"*This exceedingly interesting work. . . . Mr. Napier has certainly been well advised in admitting the general public to the knowledge of a volume which is hardly to be surpassed in point of interest among recent publications.*"—EXAMINER.

Napoleon.—THE HISTORY OF NAPOLEON I. By P. LANFREY. A Translation with the sanction of the Author. Vols. I. II. and III. 8vo. price 12*s*. each. [*Vol. IV. in the press.*

The PALL MALL GAZETTE *says it is "one of the most striking pieces of historical composition of which France has to boast," and the* SATURDAY REVIEW *calls it "an excellent translation of a work on every ground deserving to be translated. It is unquestionably and immeasurably the best that has been produced. It is in fact the only work to which we can turn for an accurate and trustworthy narrative of that extraordinary career. . . . The book is the best and indeed the only trustworthy history of Napoleon which has been written."*

Nichol.—TABLES OF EUROPEAN LITERATURE AND HISTORY, A.D. 200—1876. By J. NICHOL, LL.D., Professor of English Language and Literature, Glasgow. 4to. 6*s*. 6*d*.

TABLES OF ANCIENT LITERATURE AND HISTORY, B.C. 1500—A.D. 200. By the same Author. 4to. 4*s*. 6*d*.

Oliphant (Mrs.).—THE MAKERS OF FLORENCE: Dante Giotto, Savonarola, and their City. By Mrs. OLIPHANT. With numerous Illustrations from drawings by Professor DELAMOTTE, and portrait of Savonarola, engraved by JEENS. Second Edition. Medium 8vo. Cloth extra. 21*s*.

"*Mrs. Oliphant has made a beautiful addition to the mass of literature already piled round the records of the Tuscan capital.*"—TIMES.

"*We are grateful to Mrs. Oliphant for her eloquent and beautiful sketches of Dante, Fra Angelico, and Savonarola. They are picturesque, full of life, and rich in detail, and they are charmingly illustrated by the art of the engraver.*"—SPECTATOR.

Oliphant.—THE DUKE AND THE SCHOLAR; and other Essays. By T. L. KINGTON OLIPHANT. 8vo. 7*s*. 6*d*.

"*This volume contains one of the most beautiful biographical essays we have seen since Macaulay's days.*"—STANDARD.

Otte.—SCANDINAVIAN HISTORY. By E. C. OTTE. With Maps. Extra fcap. 8vo. 6*s*.

"*We have peculiar pleasure in recommending this intelligent résumé of Northern history as a book essential to every Englishman who interests himself in Scandinavia.*"—SPECTATOR.

Owens College Essays and Addresses.—By PROFESSORS AND LECTURERS OF OWENS COLLEGE, MANCHESTER. Published in Commemoration of the Opening of the New College Buildings, October 7th, 1873. 8vo. 14*s*.

Palgrave (R. F. D.)—THE HOUSE OF COMMONS; Illustrations of its History and Practice. By REGINALD F. D. PALGRAVE, Clerk Assistant of the House of Commons. New and Revised Edition. Crown 8vo. 2*s*. 6*d*.

Palgrave (Sir F.)—HISTORY OF NORMANDY AND OF ENGLAND. By Sir FRANCIS PALGRAVE, Deputy Keeper of Her Majesty's Public Records. Completing the History to the Death of William Rufus. 4 Vols. 8vo. 4*l.* 4*s.*

Palgrave (W. G.)—A NARRATIVE OF A YEAR'S JOURNEY THROUGH CENTRAL AND EASTERN ARABIA, 1862-3. By WILLIAM GIFFORD PALGRAVE, late of the Eighth Regiment Bombay N. I. Sixth Edition. With Maps, Plans, and Portrait of Author, engraved on steel by Jeens. Crown 8vo. 6*s.*

"*He has not only written one of the best books on the Arabs and one of the best books on Arabia, but he has done so in a manner that must command the respect no less than the admiration of his fellow-countrymen.*"—FORTNIGHTLY REVIEW.

ESSAYS ON EASTERN QUESTIONS. By W. GIFFORD PALGRAVE. 8vo. 10*s.* 6*d.*

"*These essays are full of anecdote and interest. The book is decidedly a valuable addition to the stock of literature on which men must base their opinion of the difficult social and political problems suggested by the designs of Russia, the capacity of Mahometans for sovereignty, and the good government and retention of India.*"—SATURDAY REVIEW.

DUTCH GUIANA. With Maps and Plans. 8vo. 9*s.*

"*His pages are nearly exhaustive as far as facts and statistics go, while they are lightened by graphic social sketches as well as sparkling descriptions of scenery.*"—SATURDAY REVIEW.

Patteson.—LIFE AND LETTERS OF JOHN COLERIDGE PATTESON, D.D., Missionary Bishop of the Melanesian Islands. By CHARLOTTE M. YONGE, Author of "The Heir of Redclyffe." With Portraits after RICHMOND and from Photograph, engraved by JEENS. With Map. Fifth Edition. Two Vols. Crown 8vo. 12*s.*

"*Miss Yonge's work is in one respect a model biography. It is made up almost entirely of Patteson's own letters. Aware that he had left his home once and for all, his correspondence took the form of a diary, and as we read on we come to know the man, and to love him almost as if we had seen him.*"—ATHENÆUM. "*Such a life, with its grand lessons of unselfishness, is a blessing and an honour to the age in which it is lived; the biography cannot be studied without pleasure and profit, and indeed we should think little of the man who did not rise from the study of it better and wiser. Neither the Church nor the nation which produces such sons need ever despair of its future.*"—SATURDAY REVIEW.

Pauli.—PICTURES OF OLD ENGLAND. By Dr. REINHOLD PAULI. Translated, with the approval of the Author, by E. C. OTTE. Cheaper Edition. Crown 8vo. 6*s.*

Payne.—A HISTORY OF EUROPEAN COLONIES. By E. J. PAYNE, M.A. With Maps. 18mo. 4*s*. 6*d*.

The TIMES *says:—"We have seldom met with a historian capable of forming a more comprehensive, far-seeing, and unprejudiced estimate of events and peoples, and we can commend this little work as one certain to prove of the highest interest to all thoughtful readers."*

Persia.—EASTERN PERSIA. An Account of the Journeys of the Persian Boundary Commission, 1870-1-2.—Vol. I. The Geography, with Narratives by Majors ST. JOHN, LOVETT, and EUAN SMITH, and an Introduction by Major-General Sir FREDERIC GOLDSMID, C.B., K.C.S.I., British Commissioner and Arbitrator. With Maps and Illustrations.—Vol. II. The Zoology and Geology. By W. T. BLANFORD, A.R.S.M., F.R.S. With Coloured Illustrations. Two Vols. 8vo. 42*s*.

"*The volumes largely increase our store of information about countries with which Englishmen ought to be familiar. . . . . They throw into the shade all that hitherto has appeared in our tongue respecting the local features of Persia, its scenery, its resources, even its social condition. They contain also abundant evidence of English endurance, daring, and spirit.*"—TIMES.

Prichard.—THE ADMINISTRATION OF INDIA. From 1859 to 1868. The First Ten Years of Administration under the Crown. By I. T. PRICHARD, Barrister-at-Law. Two Vols. Demy 8vo. With Map. 21*s*.

Raphael.—RAPHAEL OF URBINO AND HIS FATHER GIOVANNI SANTI. By J. D. PASSAVANT, formerly Director of the Museum at Frankfort. With Twenty Permanent Photographs. Royal 8vo. Handsomely bound. 31*s*. 6*d*.

The SATURDAY REVIEW *says of them, "We have seen not a few elegant specimens of Mr. Woodbury's new process, but we have seen none that equal these."*

Reynolds.—SIR JOSHUA REYNOLDS AS A PORTRAIT PAINTER. AN ESSAY. By J. CHURTON COLLINS, B.A. Balliol College, Oxford. Illustrated by a Series of Portraits of distinguished Beauties of the Court of George III.; reproduced in Autotype from Proof Impressions of the celebrated Engravings, by VALENTINE GREEN, THOMAS WATSON, F. R. SMITH, E. FISHER, and others. Folio half-morocco. £5 5*s*.

Rogers (James E. Thorold).—HISTORICAL GLEANINGS: A Series of Sketches. Montague, Walpole, Adam Smith, Cobbett. By Prof. ROGERS. Crown 8vo. 4*s*. 6*d*. Second Series. Wiklif, Laud, Wilkes, and Horne Tooke. Crown 8vo. 6*s*.

Routledge.—CHAPTERS IN THE HISTORY OF POPULAR PROGRESS IN ENGLAND, chiefly in Relation to the Freedom of the Press and Trial by Jury, 1660—1820. With application to later years. By J. ROUTLEDGE. 8vo. 16*s.*

"*The volume abounds in facts and information, almost always useful and often curious.*"—TIMES.

Rumford.—COUNT RUMFORD'S COMPLETE WORKS, with Memoir, and Notices of his Daughter. By GEORGE ELLIS. Five Vols. 8vo. 4*l.* 14*s.* 6*d.*

Seeley (Professor).—LECTURES AND ESSAYS. By J. R. SEELEY, M.A. Professor of Modern History in the University of Cambridge. 8vo. 10*s.* 6*d.*

CONTENTS:—*Roman Imperialism: 1. The Great Roman Revolution; 2. The Proximate Cause of the Fall of the Roman Empire; The Later Empire.—Milton's Political Opinions—Milton's Poetry—Elementary Principles in Art—Liberal Education in Universities—English in Schools—The Church as a Teacher of Morality—The Teaching of Politics: an Inaugural Lecture delivered at Cambridge.*

Shelburne.—LIFE OF WILLIAM, EARL OF SHELBURNE, AFTERWARDS FIRST MARQUIS OF LANSDOWNE. With Extracts from his Papers and Correspondence. By Lord EDMOND FITZMAURICE. In Three Vols. 8vo. Vol. I. 1737—1766, 12*s.*; Vol. II. 1766—1776, 12*s.*; Vol. III. 1776—1805. 16*s.*

"*Lord Edmond Fitzmaurice has succeeded in placing before us a wealth of new matter, which, while casting valuable and much-needed light on several obscure passages in the political history of a hundred years ago, has enabled us for the first time to form a clear and consistent idea of his ancestor.*"—SPECTATOR.

Sime.—HISTORY OF GERMANY. By JAMES SIME, M.A. 18mo. 3*s.* Being Vol. V. of the Historical Course for Schools Edited by EDWARD A. FREEMAN, D.C.L.

"*This is a remarkably clear and impressive History of Germany. Its great events are wisely kept as central figures, and the smaller events are carefully kept not only subordinate and subservient, but most skilfully woven into the texture of the historical tapestry presented to the eye.*"—STANDARD.

Squier.—PERU: INCIDENTS OF TRAVEL AND EXPLORATION IN THE LAND OF THE INCAS. By E. G. SQUIER, M.A., F.S.A., late U.S. Commissioner to Peru. With 300 Illustrations. Second Edition. 8vo. 21*s.*

The TIMES *says:*—"*No more solid and trustworthy contribution haa been made to an accurate knowledge of what are among the most wonderful ruins in the world. The work is really what its title implies. While of the greatest importance as a contribution to Peruvian archæology, it is also a thoroughly entertaining and instructive narrative of travel. Not the least important feature must be considered the numerous well executed illustrations.*"

Strangford.—EGYPTIAN SHRINES AND SYRIAN SEPULCHRES, including a Visit to Palmyra. By EMILY A. BEAUFORT (Viscountess Strangford), Author of "The Eastern Shores of the Adriatic." New Edition. Crown 8vo. *7s. 6d.*

Tait.—AN ANALYSIS OF ENGLISH HISTORY, based upon Green's "Short History of the English People." By C. W. A. TAIT, M.A., Assistant Master, Clifton College. Crown 8vo. *3s. 6d.*

Thomas.—THE LIFE OF JOHN THOMAS, Surgeon of the "Earl of Oxford" East Indiaman, and First Baptist Missionary to Bengal. By C. B. LEWIS, Baptist Missionary. 8vo. *10s. 6d.*

Thompson.—HISTORY OF ENGLAND. By EDITH THOMPSON. Being Vol. II. of the Historical Course for Schools, Edited by EDWARD A. FREEMAN, D.C.L. New Edition, revised and enlarged, with Maps. 18mo. *2s. 6d.*

"*Freedom from prejudice, simplicity of style, and accuracy of statement, are the characteristics of this volume. It is a trustworthy text-book, and likely to be generally serviceable in schools.*"—PALL MALL GAZETTE.

"*In its great accuracy and correctness of detail it stands far ahead of the general run of school manuals. Its arrangement, too, is clear, and its style simple and straightforward.*"—SATURDAY REVIEW.

Todhunter.—THE CONFLICT OF STUDIES; AND OTHER ESSAYS ON SUBJECTS CONNECTED WITH EDUCATION. By ISAAC TODHUNTER, M.A., F.R.S., late Fellow and Principal Mathematical Lecturer of St. John's College, Cambridge. 8vo. *10s. 6d.*

CONTENTS:—*I. The Conflict of Studies. II. Competitive Examinations. III. Private Study of Mathematics. IV. Academical Reform. V. Elementary Geometry. VI. The Mathematical Tripos.*

Trench (Archbishop).—For other Works by the same Author, *see* THEOLOGICAL and BELLES LETTRES CATALOGUES, and page 30 of this Catalogue.

GUSTAVUS ADOLPHUS IN GERMANY, and other Lectures on the Thirty Years' War. Second Edition, revised and enlarged. Fcap. 8vo. *4s.*

PLUTARCH, HIS LIFE, HIS LIVES, AND HIS MORALS. Five Lectures. Second Edition, enlarged. Fcap. 8vo. *3s. 6d.*

LECTURES ON MEDIEVAL CHURCH HISTORY. Being the substance of Lectures delivered in Queen's College, London. Second Edition, revised. 8vo. *12s.*

Trench (Maria).—THE LIFE OF ST. TERESA. By MARIA TRENCH. With Portrait engraved by JEENS. Crown 8vo, cloth extra. *8s. 6d.*

"*A book of rare interest.*"—JOHN BULL.

Trench (Mrs. R.)—REMAINS OF THE LATE MRS. RICHARD TRENCH. Being Selections from her Journals, Letters, and other Papers. Edited by ARCHBISHOP TRENCH. New and Cheaper Issue, with Portrait. 8vo. 6*s.*

Trollope.—A HISTORY OF THE COMMONWEALTH OF FLORENCE FROM THE EARLIEST INDEPENDENCE OF THE COMMUNE TO THE FALL OF THE REPUBLIC IN 1831. By T. ADOLPHUS TROLLOPE. 4 Vols. 8vo. Half morocco. 21*s.*

Uppingham by the Sea.—A NARRATIVE OF THE YEAR AT BORTH. By J. H. S. Crown 8vo. 3*s.* 6*d.*

Victor Emmanuel II., First King of Italy.—HIS LIFE. By G. S. GODKIN. 2 vols., crown 8vo. 16*s.*

"*An extremely clear and interesting history of one of the most important changes of later times.*"—EXAMINER.

Wallace.—THE MALAY ARCHIPELAGO: the Land of the Orang Utan and the Bird of Paradise. By ALFRED RUSSEL WALLACE. A Narrative of Travel with Studies of Man and Nature. With Maps and numerous Illustrations. Sixth Edition. Crown 8vo. 7*s.* 6*d.*

"*The result is a vivid picture of tropical life, which may be read with unflagging interest, and a sufficient account of his scientific conclusions to stimulate our appetite without wearying us by detail. In short, we may safely say that we have never read a more agreeable book of its kind.*"—SATURDAY REVIEW.

Ward.—A HISTORY OF ENGLISH DRAMATIC LITERATURE TO THE DEATH OF QUEEN ANNE. By A. W. WARD, M.A., Professor of History and English Literature in Owens College, Manchester. Two Vols. 8vo. 32*s.*

"*As full of interest as of information. To students of dramatic literature invaluable, and may be equally recommended to readers for mere pastime.*"—PALL MALL GAZETTE.

Ward (J.)—EXPERIENCES OF A DIPLOMATIST. Being recollections of Germany founded on Diaries kept during the years 1840—1870. By JOHN WARD, C.B., late H.M. Minister-Resident to the Hanse Towns. 8vo. 10*s.* 6*d.*

Waterton (C.)—WANDERINGS IN SOUTH AMERICA, THE NORTH-WEST OF THE UNITED STATES, AND THE ANTILLES IN 1812, 1816, 1820, and 1824. With Original Instructions for the perfect Preservation of Birds, etc., for Cabinets of Natural History. By CHARLES WATERTON. New Edition, edited with Biographical Introduction and Explanatory Index by the Rev. J. G. WOOD, M.A. With 100 Illustrations. 8vo. Cloth elegant. 21*s.*

Wedgwood.—JOHN WESLEY AND THE EVANGELICAL REACTION of the Eighteenth Century. By JULIA WEDGWOOD. Crown 8vo. 8*s*. 6*d*.

Whewell.—WILLIAM WHEWELL, D.D., late Master of Trinity College, Cambridge. An Account of his Writings, with Selections from his Literary and Scientific Correspondence. By I. TODHUNTER, M.A., F.R.S. Two Vols. 8vo. 25*s*.

White.—THE NATURAL HISTORY AND ANTIQUITIES OF SELBORNE. By GILBERT WHITE. Edited, with Memoir and Notes, by FRANK BUCKLAND, A Chapter on Antiquities by LORD SELBORNE, Map, &c., and numerous Illustrations by P. H. DELAMOTTE. Royal 8vo. Cloth, extra gilt. Cheaper Issue. 21*s*.

Also a Large Paper Edition, containing, in addition to the above, upwards of Thirty Woodburytype Illustrations from Drawings by Prof. DELAMOTTE. Two Vols. 4to. Half morocco, elegant. 4*l*. 4*s*.

"*Mr. Delamotte's charming illustrations are a worthy decoration of so dainty a book. They bring Selborne before us, and really help us to understand why White's love for his native place never grew cold.*"—TIMES.

Wilson.—A MEMOIR OF GEORGE WILSON, M.D., F.R.S.E., Regius Professor of Technology in the University of Edinburgh. By his SISTER. New Edition. Crown 8vo. 6*s*.

Wilson (Daniel, LL.D.)—Works by DANIEL WILSON, LL.D., Professor of History and English Literature in University College, Toronto:—

PREHISTORIC ANNALS OF SCOTLAND. New Edition, with numerous Illustrations. Two Vols. demy 8vo. 36*s*.

"*One of the most interesting, learned, and elegant works we have seen for a long time.*"—WESTMINSTER REVIEW.

PREHISTORIC MAN: Researches into the Origin of Civilization in the Old and New World. New Edition, revised and enlarged throughout, with numerous Illustrations and two Coloured Plates. Two Vols. 8vo. 36*s*.

"*A valuable work pleasantly written and well worthy of attention both by students and general readers.*"—ACADEMY.

CHATTERTON: A Biographical Study. By DANIEL WILSON, LL.D., Professor of History and English Literature in University College, Toronto. Crown 8vo. 6*s*. 6*d*.

Wyatt (Sir M. Digby).—FINE ART: a Sketch of its History, Theory, Practice, and application to Industry. A Course of Lectures delivered before the University of Cambridge. By Sir M. DIGBY WYATT, M.A. Slade Professor of Fine Art. Cheaper Issue. 8vo. 5*s.*

"*An excellent handbook for the student of art.*"—GRAPHIC. "*The book abounds in valuable matter, and will therefore be read with pleasure and profit by lovers of art.*"—DAILY NEWS.

Yonge (Charlotte M.)—Works by CHARLOTTE M. YONGE, Author of "The Heir of Redclyffe," &c., &c. :—

A PARALLEL HISTORY OF FRANCE AND ENGLAND: consisting of Outlines and Dates. Oblong 4to. 3*s.* 6*d.*

CAMEOS FROM ENGLISH HISTORY. From Rollo to Edward II. Extra fcap. 8vo. Third Edition. 5*s.*

SECOND SERIES, THE WARS IN FRANCE. Extra fcap. 8vo. Third Edition. 5*s.*

THIRD SERIES, THE WARS OF THE ROSES. Extra fcap. 8vo. 5*s.*

"*Instead of dry details,*" *says the* NONCONFORMIST, "*we have living pictures, faithful, vivid, and striking.*"

FOURTH SERIES. [*Nearly ready.*

HISTORY OF FRANCE. Maps. 18mo. 3*s.* 6*d.* [*Historical Course for Schools.*

POLITICS, POLITICAL AND SOCIAL ECONOMY, LAW, AND KINDRED SUBJECTS.

Anglo-Saxon Law.—ESSAYS IN. Contents: Law Courts —Land and Family Laws and Legal Procedure generally. With Select cases. Medium 8vo. 18*s*.

Arnold.—THE ROMAN SYSTEM OF PROVINCIAL ADMINISTRATION TO THE ACCESSION OF CONSTANTINE THE GREAT. Being the Arnold Prize Essay for 1879. By W. T. Arnold, B.A. Crown 8vo. 6*s*.

Ball.—THE STUDENT'S GUIDE TO THE BAR. By WALTER W. BALL, M.A., of the Inner Temple, Barrister-at-Law. Crown 8vo. 2*s*. 6*d*.

"*The student will here find a clear statement of the several steps by which the degree of barrister is obtained, and also useful advice about the advantages of a prolonged course of 'reading in Chambers.'*"—ACADEMY.

Bernard.—FOUR LECTURES ON SUBJECTS CONNECTED WITH DIPLOMACY. BY MONTAGUE BERNARD, M.A., Chichele Professor of International Law and Diplomacy, Oxford. 8vo. 9*s*.

"*Singularly interesting lectures, so able, clear, and attractive.*"—SPECTATOR.

Bright (John, M.P.)—Works by the Right Hon. JOHN BRIGHT, M.P.

SPEECHES ON QUESTIONS OF PUBLIC POLICY. Edited by Professor THOROLD ROGERS. Author's Popular Edition. Globe 8vo. 3*s*. 6*d*.

"*Mr. Bright's speeches will always deserve to be studied, as an apprenticeship to popular and parliamentary oratory; they will form materials for the history of our time, and many brilliant passages, perhaps some entire speeches, will really become a part of the living literature of England.*"—DAILY NEWS.

LIBRARY EDITION. Two Vols. 8vo. With Portrait. 25*s*.

PUBLIC ADDRESSES. Edited by J. THOROLD ROGERS. 8vo. 14*s*.

Bucknill.—HABITUAL DRUNKENNESS AND INSANE DRUNKARDS. By J. C. BUCKNILL, M.D., F.R.S., late Lord Chancellor's Visitor of Lunatics. Crown 8vo. 2*s*. 6*d*.

Cairnes.—Works by J. E. CAIRNES, M.A., Emeritus Professor of Political Economy in University College, London.

ESSAYS IN POLITICAL ECONOMY, THEORETICAL and APPLIED. By J. E. CAIRNES, M.A., Professor of Political Economy in University College, London. 8vo. 10*s*. 6*d*.

POLITICAL ESSAYS. 8vo. 10*s*. 6*d*.

SOME LEADING PRINCIPLES OF POLITICAL ECONOMY NEWLY EXPOUNDED. 8vo. 14*s*.

CONTENTS :—*Part I. Value. Part II. Labour and Capital. Part III. International Trade.*

"*A work which is perhaps the most valuable contribution to the science made since the publication, a quarter of a century since, of Mr. Mill's 'Principles of Political Economy.'*"—DAILY NEWS.

THE CHARACTER AND LOGICAL METHOD OF POLITICAL ECONOMY. New Edition, enlarged. 8vo. 7*s*. 6*d*.

"*These lectures are admirably fitted to correct the slipshod generalizations which pass current as the science of Political Economy.*"—TIMES.

Clarke.—EARLY ROMAN LAW. THE REGAL PERIOD. By E. C. CLARKE, M.A., of Lincoln's Inn, Barrister-at-Law, Lecturer in Law and Regius Professor of Civil Law at Cambridge. Crown 8vo. 5*s*.

Cobden (Richard).—SPEECHES ON QUESTIONS OF PUBLIC POLICY. By RICHARD COBDEN. Edited by the Right Hon. John Bright, M.P., and J. E. Thorold Rogers. Popular Edition. 8vo. 3*s*. 6*d*.

Fawcett.—Works by HENRY FAWCETT, M.A., M.P., Fellow of Trinity Hall, and Professor of Political Economy in the University of Cambridge :—

THE ECONOMIC POSITION OF THE BRITISH LABOURER. Extra fcap. 8vo. 5*s*.

MANUAL OF POLITICAL ECONOMY. Fifth Edition, with New Chapters on the Depreciation of Silver, etc. Crown 8vo. 12*s*.

The DAILY NEWS *says:* "*It forms one of the best introductions to the principles of the science, and to its practical applications in the problems of modern, and especially of English, government and society.*"

PAUPERISM: ITS CAUSES AND REMEDIES. Crown 8vo. 5*s*. 6*d*.

The ATHENÆUM *calls the work* "*a repertory of interesting and well digested information.*"

SPEECHES ON SOME CURRENT POLITICAL QUESTIONS. 8vo. 10*s*. 6*d*.

"*They will help to educate, not perhaps, parties, but the educators of parties.*"—DAILY NEWS.

Fawcett.—*continued.*

ESSAYS ON POLITICAL AND SOCIAL SUBJECTS. By PROFESSOR FAWCETT, M.P., and MILLICENT GARRETT FAWCETT. 8vo. 10*s.* 6*d.*

"*They will all repay the perusal of the thinking reader.*"—DAILY NEWS.

FREE TRADE AND PROTECTION: an Inquiry into the Causes which have retarded the general adoption of Free Trade since its introduction into England. Third Edition. 8vo. 7*s.* 6*d.*

"*No greater service can be rendered to the cause of Free Trade than a clear explanation of the principles on which Free Trade rests. Professor Fawcett has done this in the volume before us with all his habitual clearness of thought and expression.*"—ECONOMIST.

Fawcett (Mrs.)—Works by MILLICENT GARRETT FAWCETT.

POLITICAL ECONOMY FOR BEGINNERS. WITH QUESTIONS. New Edition. 18mo. 2*s.* 6*d.*

The DAILY NEWS *calls it "clear, compact, and comprehensive;" and the* SPECTATOR *says, "Mrs. Fawcett's treatise is perfectly suited to its purpose."*

TALES IN POLITICAL ECONOMY. Crown 8vo. 3*s.*

"*The idea is a good one, and it is quite wonderful what a mass of economic teaching the author manages to compress into a small space... The true doctrines of International Trade, Currency, and the ratio between Production and Population, are set before us and illustrated in a masterly manner.*"—ATHENÆUM.

Freeman (E. A.), M.A., D.C.L.—COMPARATIVE POLITICS. Lectures at the Royal Institution, to which is added "The Unity of History," being the Rede Lecture delivered at Cambridge in 1872. 8vo. 14*s.*

"*We find in Mr. Freeman's new volume the same sound, careful, comprehensive qualities which have long ago raised him to so high a place amongst historical writers. For historical discipline, then, as well as historical information, Mr. Freeman's book is full of value.*"—PALL MALL GAZETTE.

Goschen.—REPORTS AND SPEECHES ON LOCAL TAXATION. By GEORGE J. GOSCHEN, M.P. Royal 8vo. 5*s.*

"*The volume contains a vast mass of information of the highest value.*" —ATHENÆUM.

Guide to the Unprotected, in Every Day Matters Relating to Property and Income. By a BANKER'S DAUGHTER. Fourth Edition, Revised. Extra fcap. 8vo. 3*s.* 6*d.*

"*Many an unprotected female will bless the head which planned and the hand which compiled this admirable little manual. . . . This book was very much wanted, and it could not have been better done.*"—MORNING STAR.

Hamilton.—MONEY AND VALUE: an Inquiry into the Means and Ends of Economic Production, with an Appendix on the Depreciation of Silver and Indian Currency. By ROWLAND HAMILTON. 8vo. 12*s.*

"*The subject is here dealt with in a luminous style, and by presenting it from a new point of view in connection with the nature and functions of money, a genuine service has been rendered to commercial science.*"—BRITISH QUARTERLY REVIEW.

Harwood.—DISESTABLISHMENT: a Defence of the Principle of a National Church. By GEORGE HARWOOD, M.A. 8vo. 12*s.*

Hill.—Works by OCTAVIA HILL:—

HOMES OF THE LONDON POOR. Extra fcap. 8vo. 3*s.* 6*d.*
"*She is clear, practical, and definite.*"—GLOBE.

OUR COMMON LAND; and other Short Essays. Extra fcap. 8vo. 3*s.* 6*d.*

CONTENTS:—*Our Common Land. District Visiting. A More Excellent Way of Charity. A Word on Good Citizenship. Open Spaces. Effectual Charity. The Future of our Commons.*

Historicus.—LETTERS ON SOME QUESTIONS OF INTERNATIONAL LAW. Reprinted from the *Times*, with considerable Additions. 8vo. 7*s.* 6*d.* Also, ADDITIONAL LETTERS. 8vo. 2*s.* 6*d.*

Holland.—THE TREATY RELATIONS OF RUSSIA AND TURKEY FROM 1774 TO 1853. A Lecture delivered at Oxford, April 1877. By T. E. HOLLAND, D.C.L., Professor of International Law and Diplomacy, Oxford. Crown 8vo. 2*s.*

Hughes (Thos.)—THE OLD CHURCH: WHAT SHALL WE DO WITH IT? By THOMAS HUGHES, Q.C. Crown 8vo. 6*s.*

Jevons.—Works by W. STANLEY JEVONS, M.A., Professor of Political Economy in University College, London. (For other Works by the same Author, *see* EDUCATIONAL and PHILOSOPHICAL CATALOGUES.)

THE COAL QUESTION: An Inquiry Concerning the Progress of the Nation, and the Probable Exhaustion of our Coal Mines. Second Edition, revised. 8vo. 10*s.* 6*d.*

Jevons.—*continued.*

THE THEORY OF POLITICAL ECONOMY. Second Edition, revised, with new Preface and Appendices. 8vo. 10*s.* 6*d.*

"*Professor Jevons has done invaluable service by courageously claiming political economy to be strictly a branch of Applied Mathematics.*" —WESTMINSTER REVIEW.

PRIMER OF POLITICAL ECONOMY. 18mo. 1*s.*

Laveleye. — PRIMITIVE PROPERTY. By EMILE DE LAVELEYE. Translated by G. R. L. MARRIOTT, LL.B., with an Introduction by T. E. CLIFFE LESLIE, LL.B. 8vo. 12*s.*

"*It is almost impossible to over-estimate the value of the well-digested knowledge which it contains; it is one of the most learned books that have been contributed to the historical department of the literature of economic science.*"—ATHENÆUM.

Leading Cases done into English. By an APPRENTICE OF LINCOLN'S INN. Third Edition. Crown 8vo. 2*s.* 6*d.*

"*Here is a rare treat for the lovers of quaint conceits, who in reading this charming little book will find enjoyment in the varied metre and graphic language in which the several tales are told, no less than in the accurate and pithy rendering of some of our most familiar 'Leading Cases.'*"—SATURDAY REVIEW.

Lubbock.—ADDRESSES, POLITICAL AND EDUCATIONAL. By Sir JOHN LUBBOCK, Bart., M.P., &c., &c. 8vo, pp. 209. 8*s.* 6*d.*

The ten speeches given are (1) on the Imperial Policy of Great Britain, (2) on the Bank Act of 1844, (3) on the Present System of Public School Education, 1876, (4) on the Present System of Elementary Education, (5) on the Income Tax, (6) on the National Debt, (7) on the Declaration of Paris, (8) on Marine Insurances, (9) on the Preservation of Ancient Monuments, and (10) on Egypt.

Macdonell.—THE LAND QUESTION, WITH SPECIAL REFERENCE TO ENGLAND AND SCOTLAND. By JOHN MACDONELL, Barrister-at-Law. 8vo. 10*s.* 6*d.*

Martin.—THE STATESMAN'S YEAR-BOOK: A Statistical and Historical Annual of the States of the Civilized World, for the year 1879. By FREDERICK MARTIN. Sixteenth Annual Publication. Revised after Official Returns. Crown 8vo. 10*s.* 6*d.*

The Statesman's Year-Book is the only work in the English language which furnishes a clear and concise account of the actual condition of all the States of Europe, the civilized countries of America, Asia, and

Africa, and the British Colonies and Dependencies in all parts of the world. The new issue of the work has been revised and corrected, on the basis of official reports received direct from the heads of the leading Governments of the world, in reply to letters sent to them by the Editor. Through the valuable assistance thus given, it has been possible to collect an amount of information, political, statistical, and commercial, of the latest date, and of unimpeachable trustworthiness, such as no publication of the same kind has ever been able to furnish. "As indispensable as Bradshaw."—TIMES.

Monahan.—THE METHOD OF LAW: an Essay on the Statement and Arrangement of the Legal Standard of Conduct. By J. H. MONAHAN, Q.C. Crown 8vo. 6*s*.

"*Will be found valuable by careful law students who have felt the importance of gaining clear ideas regarding the relations between the parts of the complex organism they have to study.*"—BRITISH QUARTERLY REVIEW.

Paterson.—THE LIBERTY OF THE SUBJECT AND THE LAWS OF ENGLAND RELATING TO THE SECURITY OF THE PERSON. Commentaries on. By JAMES PATERSON, M.A., Barrister at Law, sometime Commissioner for English and Irish Fisheries, etc. Cheaper issue. Two Vols. Crown 8vo. 21*s*.

"*Two or three hours' dipping into these volumes, not to say reading them through, will give legislators and stump orators a knowledge of the liberty of a citizen of their country, in its principles, its fulness, and its modification, such as they probably in nine cases out of ten never had before.*"—SCOTSMAN.

Phillimore.—PRIVATE LAW AMONG THE ROMANS, from the Pandects. By JOHN GEORGE PHILLIMORE, Q.C. 8vo. 16*s*.

Rogers.—COBDEN AND POLITICAL OPINION. By J. E. THOROLD ROGERS. 8vo. 10*s*. 6*d*.

"*Will be found most useful by politicians of every school, as it forms a sort of handbook to Cobden's teaching.*"—ATHENÆUM.

Stephen (C. E.)—THE SERVICE OF THE POOR; Being an Inquiry into the Reasons for and against the Establishment of Religious Sisterhoods for Charitable Purposes. By CAROLINE EMILIA STEPHEN. Crown 8vo. 6*s*. 6*d*.

"*The ablest advocate of a better line of work in this direction that we have ever seen.*"—EXAMINER.

Stephen.—Works by Sir JAMES F. STEPHEN, K.C.S.I., Q.C.

A DIGEST OF THE LAW OF EVIDENCE. Third Edition with New Preface. Crown 8vo. 6*s*.

Stephen.—*continued.*

A DIGEST OF THE CRIMINAL LAW. (Crimes and Punishments.) 8vo. 16*s.*

"*We feel sure that any person of ordinary intelligence who had never looked into a law-book in his life might, by a few days' careful study of this volume, obtain a more accurate understanding of the criminal law, a more perfect conception of its different bearings a more thorough and intelligent insight into its snares and pitfalls, than an ordinary practitioner can boast of after years of study of the ordinary text-books and practical experience of the Courts unassisted by any competent guide.*"—SATURDAY REVIEW.

A GENERAL VIEW OF THE CRIMINAL LAW OF ENGLAND. Two Vols. Crown 8vo. [*New edition in the press.*

Stubbs.—VILLAGE POLITICS. Addresses and Sermons on the Labour Question. By C. W. STUBBS, M.A., Vicar of Granborough, Bucks. Extra fcap. 8vo. 3*s.* 6*d.*

Thornton.—Works by W. T. THORNTON, C.B., Secretary for Public Works in the India Office :—

ON LABOUR: Its Wrongful Claims and Rightful Dues; Its Actual Present and Possible Future. Second Edition, revised, 8vo. 14*s.*

A PLEA FOR PEASANT PROPRIETORS: With the Outlines of a Plan for their Establishment in Ireland. New Edition, revised. Crown 8vo. 7*s.* 6*d.*

INDIAN PUBLIC WORKS AND COGNATE INDIAN TOPICS. With Map of Indian Railways. Crown 8vo. 8*s.* 6*d.*

Walker.—Works by F. A. WALKER, M.A., Ph.D., Professor of Political Economy and History, Yale College :—

THE WAGES QUESTION. A Treatise on Wages and the Wages Class. 8vo. 14*s.*

MONEY. 8vo. 16*s.*

"*It is painstaking, laborious, and states the question in a clear and very intelligible form. . . . The volume possesses a great value as a sort of encyclopædia of knowledge on the subject.*"—ECONOMIST.

Work about the Five Dials. With an Introductory Note by THOMAS CARLYLE. Crown 8vo. 6*s.*

"*A book which abounds with wise and practical suggestions.*"—PALL MALL GAZETTE.

WORKS CONNECTED WITH THE SCIENCE OR THE HISTORY OF LANGUAGE.

Abbott.—A SHAKESPERIAN GRAMMAR: An Attempt to illustrate some of the Differences between Elizabethan and Modern English. By the Rev. E. A. ABBOTT, D.D., Head Master of the City of London School. New and Enlarged Edition. Extra fcap. 8vo. 6*s.*

"*Valuable not only as an aid to the critical study of Shakespeare, but as tending to familiarize the reader with Elizabethan English in general.*"—ATHENÆUM.

Besant.—STUDIES IN EARLY FRENCH POETRY. By WALTER BESANT, M.A. Crown 8vo. 8*s.* 6*d.*

Breymann.—A FRENCH GRAMMAR BASED ON PHILOLOGICAL PRINCIPLES. By HERMANN BREYMANN, Ph.D., Professor of Philology in the University of Munich late Lecturer on French Language and Literature at Owens College, Manchester. Extra fcap. 8vo. 4*s.* 6*d.*

"*We dismiss the work with every feeling of satisfaction. It cannot fail to be taken into use by all schools which endeavour to make the study of French a means towards the higher culture.*"—EDUCATIONAL TIMES.

Ellis.—PRACTICAL HINTS ON THE QUANTITATIVE PRONUNCIATION OF LATIN, FOR THE USE OF CLASSICAL TEACHERS AND LINGUISTS. By A. J. ELLIS, B.A., F.R.S., &c. Extra fcap. 8vo. 4*s.* 6*d.*

Fleay.—A SHAKESPEARE MANUAL. By the Rev. F. G. FLEAY, M.A., Head Master of Skipton Grammar School. Extra fcap. 8vo. 4*s.* 6*d.*

Goodwin.—SYNTAX OF THE GREEK MOODS AND TENSES. By W. W. GOODWIN, Professor of Greek Literature in Harvard University. New Edition. Crown 8vo. 6*s.* 6*d.*

Hadley.—ESSAYS PHILOLOGICAL AND CRITICAL. Selected from the Papers of JAMES HADLEY, LL.D., Professor of Greek in Yale College, &c. 8vo. 16*s.*

Hales.—LONGER ENGLISH POEMS. With Notes, Philological and Explanatory, and an Introduction on the Teaching of English. Chiefly for use in Schools. Edited by J. W. HALES, M.A., Professor of English Literature at King's College, London, &c. &c. Fifth Edition. Extra fcap. 8vo. 4*s.* 6*d.*

Helfenstein (James).—A COMPARATIVE GRAMMAR OF THE TEUTONIC LANGUAGES: Being at the same time a Historical Grammar of the English Language, and comprising Gothic, Anglo-Saxon, Early English, Modern English, Icelandic (Old Norse), Danish, Swedish, Old High German, Middle High German, Modern German, Old Saxon, Old Frisian, and Dutch. By JAMES HELFENSTEIN, Ph.D. 8vo. 18*s.*

Masson (Gustave).—A COMPENDIOUS DICTIONARY OF THE FRENCH LANGUAGE (French-English and English-French). Followed by a List of the Principal Diverging Derivations, and preceded by Chronological and Historical Tables. By GUSTAVE MASSON, Assistant-Master and Librarian, Harrow School. Fourth Edition. Crown 8vo. Half-bound. 6*s.*

"*A book which any student, whatever may be the degree of his advancement in the language, would do well to have on the table close at hand while he is reading.*"—SATURDAY REVIEW.

Mayor.—A BIBLIOGRAPHICAL CLUE TO LATIN LITERATURE. Edited after Dr. E. HUBNER. With large Additions by JOHN E. B. MAYOR, M.A., Professor of Latin in the University of Cambridge. Crown 8vo. 6*s.* 6*d.*

"*An extremely useful volume that should be in the hands of all scholars.*"—ATHENÆUM.

Morris.—Works by the Rev. RICHARD MORRIS, LL.D., Member of the Council of the Philol. Soc., Lecturer on English Language and Literature in King's College School, Editor of "Specimens of Early English," etc., etc.:—

HISTORICAL OUTLINES OF ENGLISH ACCIDENCE, comprising Chapters on the History and Development of the Language, and on Word-formation. Sixth Edition. Fcap. 8vo. 6*s.*

ELEMENTARY LESSONS IN HISTORICAL ENGLISH GRAMMAR, containing Accidence and Word-formation. Third Edition. 18mo. 2*s.* 6*d.*

Oliphant.—THE OLD AND MIDDLE ENGLISH. By T. L. KINGTON OLIPHANT, M.A., of Balliol College, Oxford. A New Edition, revised and greatly enlarged, of "The Sources of Standard English." Extra fcap. 8vo. 9*s.*

"*Mr. Oliphant's book is, to our mind, one of the ablest and most scholarly contributions to our standard English we have seen for many years.*"—SCHOOL BOARD CHRONICLE. "*The book comes nearer to a history of the English language than anything we have seen since such a history could be written, without confusion and contradictions.*"—SATURDAY REVIEW.

Peile (John, M.A.)—AN INTRODUCTION TO GREEK AND LATIN ETYMOLOGY. By JOHN PEILE, M.A., Fellow and Tutor of Christ's College, Cambridge. Third and revised Edition. Crown 8vo. 10*s.* 6*d.*

"*The book may be accepted as a very valuable contribution to the science of language.*"—SATURDAY REVIEW.

Philology.—THE JOURNAL OF SACRED AND CLASSICAL PHILOLOGY. Four Vols. 8vo. 12*s.* 6*d.* each.

THE JOURNAL OF PHILOLOGY. New Series. Edited by JOHN E. B. MAYOR, M.A., and W. ALDIS WRIGHT, M.A. 4*s.* 6*d.* (Half-yearly.)

Roby (H. J.)—A GRAMMAR OF THE LATIN LANGUAGE, FROM PLAUTUS TO SUETONIUS. By HENRY JOHN ROBY, M.A., late Fellow of St. John's College, Cambridge. In Two Parts. Second Edition. Part I. containing:—Book I. Sounds. Book II. Inflexions. Book III. Word Formation. Appendices. Crown 8vo. 8*s.* 6*d.* Part II.—Syntax, Prepositions, &c. Crown 8vo. 10*s.* 6*d.*

"*The book is marked by the clear and practical insight of a master in his art. It is a book which would do honour to any country.*"—ATHENÆUM. "*Brings before the student in a methodical form the best results of modern philology bearing on the Latin language.*"—SCOTSMAN.

Schmidt.—THE RYTHMIC AND METRIC OF THE CLASSICAL LANGUAGES. To which are added, the Lyric Parts of the "Medea" of Euripides and the "Antigone" of Sophocles; with Rhythmical Scheme and Commentary. By Dr. J. H. SCHMIDT. Translated from the German by J. W. WHITE, D.D. 8vo. 10*s.* 6*d.*

Taylor.—Works by the Rev. ISAAC TAYLOR, M.A.:—

ETRUSCAN RESEARCHES. With Woodcuts. 8vo. 14*s.*

The TIMES *says:—"The learning and industry displayed in this volume deserve the most cordial recognition. The ultimate verdict of science we shall not attempt to anticipate; but we can safely say this, that it is a learned book which the unlearned can enjoy, and that in the descriptions of the tomb-builders, as well as in the marvellous coincidences and unexpected analogies brought together by the author, readers of every grade may take delight as well as philosophers and scholars.*"

WORDS AND PLACES; or, Etymological Illustrations of History, Ethnology, and Geography. By the Rev. ISAAC TAYLOR. Third Edition, revised and compressed. With Maps. Globe 8vo. 6*s.*

GREEKS AND GOTHS: a Study on the Runes. 8vo. 9*s.*

Trench.—Works by R. CHENEVIX TRENCH, D.D., Archbishop of Dublin. (For other Works by the same Author, *see* THEOLOGICAL CATALOGUE.)

SYNONYMS OF THE NEW TESTAMENT. Eighth Edition, enlarged. 8vo, cloth. 12*s.*

"*He is,*" *the* ATHENÆUM *says,* "*a guide in this department of knowledge to whom his readers may entrust themselves with confidence.*"

ON THE STUDY OF WORDS. Lectures Addressed (originally) to the Pupils at the Diocesan Training School, Winchester. Seventeenth Edition, enlarged. Fcap. 8vo. 5*s.*

ENGLISH PAST AND PRESENT. Tenth Edition, revised and improved. Fcap. 8vo. 5*s.*

A SELECT GLOSSARY OF ENGLISH WORDS USED FORMERLY IN SENSES DIFFERENT FROM THEIR PRESENT. Fourth Edition, enlarged. Fcap. 8vo. 4*s.*

Whitney.—A COMPENDIOUS GERMAN GRAMMAR. By W. D. WHITNEY, Professor of Sanskrit and Instructor in Modern Languages in Yale College. Crown 8vo. 6*s.*

"*After careful examination we are inclined to pronounce it the best grammar of modern language we have ever seen.*"—SCOTSMAN.

Whitney and Edgren.—A COMPENDIOUS GERMAN AND ENGLISH DICTIONARY, with Notation of Correspondences and Brief Etymologies. By Professor W. D. WHITNEY, assisted by A. H. EDGREN. Crown 8vo. 7*s.* 6*d.*

The GERMAN-ENGLISH Part may be had separately. Price 5*s.*

Yonge.—HISTORY OF CHRISTIAN NAMES. By CHARLOTTE M. YONGE, Author of "The Heir of Redclyffe." Cheaper Edition. Two Vols. Crown 8vo. 12*s.*

www.ingramcontent.com/pod-product-compliance
Lightning Source LLC
Chambersburg PA
CBHW021529210326
41599CB00012B/1434

* 9 7 8 3 7 4 2 8 3 9 5 6 5 *